REALIGN with *Joy*

A Transformational Path to Self and Creativity

ANGELA ANDERSON

Edited by Amy Delcambre
Cover Design by: Kristina Edstrom

PEAK PRESS

An Imprint for GracePoint Publishing (www.GracePointPublishing.com)

GracePoint Matrix, LLC
624 S. Cascade Ave, Suite 201
Colorado Springs, CO 80903
www.GracePointMatrix.com
Email: Admin@GracePointMatrix.com

SAN # 991-6032

A Library of Congress Control Number has been requested and is pending.

ISBN: (Paperback) 978-1-961347-69-4
eISBN: 978-1-961347-70-0

Books may be purchased for educational, business, or sales promotional use.
For bulk order requests and price schedule contact:
Orders@GracePointPublishing.com

Table of Contents

Dedication

Thank you to my parents for all that you have and have not done. Thank you for your support and encouragement and for allowing me to follow my different paths.

Thank you to the team at GracePoint for making a dream a reality. Special thanks to my developmental editor Amy, who helped me completely transform this book into something to be proud of.

Thank you to my team in spirit and ancestors. Thank you to the healing presence and beauty of nature and animals. My deepest gratitude goes to my most awesome teacher and mentor, Tiama (my horse), who initiated and carried me through much of my healing, kept me grounded on the road of realignment, and brought me back to myself.

My most joyous memories are of Tiama galloping (especially to me) and watching her and the sunset whist listening to her eat.

Realign with Joy

Joy Full Self

Joy is not found in things outside of you

    although they may help you observe it.

Joy is not in circumstances or other people

    although they may help you connect with it.

Joy is not happiness, nor an emotion or sentiment;

    joy is a state of being, a state of love.

Joy can be felt, even when sad or grieving;

    joy is enduring, where emotions are fleeting.

Happiness and sadness are waves;

    joy is the ocean and Source.

Joy is not something you can work on, nor discover;

    it discovers you.

Joy is not what we think it is;

    as joy is not found in the mind

Joy resides in the heart and the body;

    coursing through your blood and veins.

Joy is always waiting to rise within you

... when you stop striving... when you are you.

Joy is vitality that draws and coaches you forward

through heartfelt dreams and wishes.

Joy fills you up and resonates;

joy is serene and feels like home.

When you connect with the joy within

nothing and nobody can displace it.

Joy is an essential part of self.

Joy is a symptom of being aligned with you.

Joy is the gift given with your birth,

have you unwrapped and opened it?

Joy

Opens

You   ... to your divine *real* Self.

Introduction:

Joyous Self

Joy is what we feel when we feel connected, whether it is with the many aspects of ourselves or feeling connected with family, friends, community, pets, nature, earth, or spirit...it does not matter. It is joy-o-us, not joy-o-me. We are designed to live in relationship, not isolation.

Our greatest need (of which joy is a side effect) is the feeling of belonging and that we have the freedom to be (or become) who we truly are (and be accepted as we are). We may be at our most joyous when we are connected authentically through relationships and creativity. Our most joyous relationship (hopefully) is with self and life; however, it does not always work out or feel that way.

Though strange to say, freedom and joy may be our greatest fears, but that's because we have developed many ways during our lives to limit both freedom and joy. We may feel more comfortable with the familiarity of discomfort, working hard and feeling "less than," rather than feeling full with joyful ease. We limit, put up obstacles, and put off joy and happiness every time we think or say, "I will be happy when _____." Yet, you most likely know you may not be sustainably happier or joyous when you do get it. Sometimes there is joy initially, although not guaranteed. How long does it take for the happiness or joy to wear off?

Why wait to be happy or joyous? Why not now? What can you do to shift the spell of the uncomfortable familiarity of feeling *blah*? It may be as simple as becoming aware and pausing for a moment or taking a few deep breaths or giving yourself a smile, a hug, or a wink. Being in nature or seeing the beauty in something may also break the spell.

We gain true wisdom through embodying thoughts and beliefs aligned for you via action and experience, and this is why so many exercises are included in this book. Theory helps a person gain understanding; however, applying theory through action is powerful as it moves and changes energy.

First and foremost, this book aims to assist or guide you in realigning your connection with yourself. To change the world, you need to change "the world of you." When you realign the relationship with yourself, it changes how you relate with the world as the world rushes in to meet you. Becoming more aligned within yourself means you also become more tuned in to receiving feedback from the world. You are better able to read, learn, respond, and relate in relationships and to events more intuitively, efficiently, and effectively. Change your perspective and how you respond to the world, and you change what you see and how you experience the world. It all starts with *you.*

You were born with innate gifts and talents; it is your genius in your genes. Your *gen(e)-I-us* is your genetic gift of your uniqueness (I) that is to be shared with others (us). Your genius is the most joyous expression of you. You come into this world with a unique purpose *and* with all the necessary gifts and talents to fulfil, express, and share with others. You have access to everything you need and whether you share that with one or many, it ripples out to the whole as we are all connected.

I hope this book helps reconnect you with yourself so you can experience your genius and joy. The world needs you to fill the space of you in order to be your unique contribution to the world, simply through being your joyful self.

How Do We Lose Our Joy?

What led to writing this book was the exploration that happened after asking my parents, "What was I like as a baby?" I had not been expecting to hear "joyful and loving" as my instant internal reaction was, *What the fuck happened?* Joyful and loving felt quite far from my reality for much of my life.

I did not necessarily have a bad childhood, although in my youth I would have said it was. Extreme sensitivities and autism (unknown at the time) made life experiences harsh, intense, and more challenging; I felt sad, angry, and like I didn't fit in. Looking back at the themes I have worked on during my adult life—shyness, anger, depression, sensitivities, addiction, fatigue, burnout, perfectionism, inadequacy, human suffering, wounding, victimisation, self-abandonment, lack of confidence, low self-esteem, and trying to prove myself, just to name a few—I guess I *do* know what happened: navigating life and growing up happened.

If joy (and love) is an innate state and something we are born with (or as), what causes us to deviate from or lose this joy? And how do we find or reconnect with that joy again?

My most joyful memories as a child usually involved feeling the connection with animals and nature including skipping barefoot through the paddocks with my dog, singing to the cows, sheep, and birds, and hearing the birds sing back along with a few appreciative *baas* and *moos*. Warm spring days with misty rain decorating cobwebbed fences like magical fairy lights and delicate chandeliers delighted me. I took pleasure in riding my horse bareback with only a halter (and not even that sometimes), watching animals graze, walking with or being followed by dogs, lambs, calves, and horses, and snuggling with my sleeping horse, dog, or cat. Many joyful memories involved animals. Even as an adult, simply being with, watching, or listening to my horse eat have been my favourite and most precious moments, especially when accompanied by a spectacular sunrise or sunset.

Unfortunately, Western culture and society place more importance on doing than being, on thinking than feeling, and on defence and attack than peace and surrender. We live and grow up with negative bias, where sensitivity and feelings are considered weaknesses. As we stop or avoid feeling the negative feelings, it also blocks us from feeling the positive. We give up the bad and the good. As we learn to protect and separate ourselves from our feelings, we also create barriers to joy in order to fit in or obtain a false sense of safety.

Negative bias is not all bad; it is an effective survival adaptation. We look out for, observe, and share (ideally as fact, without fault or blame) the unsafe, risky, or negative things going on around us, so others do not have to suffer the same. Negativity is shared conditioning that ensures survival. However, what threatens our survival today is *very* different from what threatened us when these negative biases were first laid down. Today the stress of these negative biases may be our greatest threat and limitation.

For those of us lucky enough to live in places not at war, threats and stresses can be more theoretical in origin, rather than physical or actual. Today unintegrated trauma, and uninvestigated or unquestioned thoughts and feelings threaten and influence how we are in the world.

At the root of all violence, division, and war is unintegrated hurt, pain, or trauma, which results in us caring less about ourselves, others, the environment, and the world. People who hurt others are people who have been hurt and are hurting. Bullies were first bullied. To realign and stop the cycle, we need to stop punishing and find compassion for the origin of that hurt.

We have been taught to suppress, limit, restrict, distrust, and even fear our emotions, joy, or bliss. As a child you might remember some or all of the following:

- blissfully staring out the window immersed in the wonder and awe of a bird, tree, sky, or cloud... and being shocked back into paying attention;
- joyfully and maybe rambunctiously playing with friends, siblings, or others and being told to "stop being silly" or that "it is all fun until someone gets hurt";
- delightfully sharing a creative or ingenious discovery, invention, drawing, painting, poem, story, song, dance, solution, or idea only to be told to stop or have it ignored, dismissed, ridiculed, critiqued, improved, teased, joked about, or had all the joy sucked out of it;
- ecstatically expressing your joy about something, and being punished or told to settle, calm down, or stop being "too much";
- being asked to explain why you are so happy or joyful, which took you out of your feelings and into your head, cutting the connection and flow that was beyond words;
- being told your ideas or behaviour were wrong or inappropriate, because of political correctness, or because they conflicted with, challenged, or made another feel uncomfortable or triggered; and
- being tickled as a form of torture or to the extent you feared losing control or could no longer connect with its delight.

Many things that connect us with our emotions and with our joy are disciplined, trained, or punished out of us. The deeper the "good" or "bad" emotions are suppressed or buried, the more difficult it can be for joy to rise up.

Your Invitation

This book is intended as a guide, not an instruction manual. It comes with an invitation to explore what is and is not correct and aligned with and for *you*.

I invite you to approach this book (and life) with childlike wonder and curiosity. Allow yourself to let go of thinking you know how things are and how they work (and I am not saying I think I know either). Take sips from this book. If you need to consume it all in one go, come back to do some of the exercises.

Although there is order in reading the book front to back, you may want to use it like a reference, guide, or oracle when you are seeking clarity by randomly selecting a page, chapter, part, or exercise. You may want to scan the table of contents, or appendix of exercises and see what pops or stands out. If you need further information on any concepts, it might be found in previous sections of the book.

Play with the ideas in this book and see if and how they fit. Let the book *and* your imagination take you on an adventure. Allow the possibility of inspiration, delight, and joy to arise. Take notice of how you feel and what things feel good. Tune in to what feels aligned and true for you, as we do not all share the same truths.

When doing the exercises, find the place where you can simply allow and not judge things as right or wrong or as a mistake. Find your truth by simply considering things as experiences that feel aligned... or not.

Practices and exercises feel different depending on your mood and what is happening. You may dislike an exercise or think an exercise is useless one day and be blown away on another, so I invite you to revisit (you will find all the realigning exercises listed in the appendix).

If you are new to these topics, parts may feel overwhelming at times, as they challenge your current beliefs and perspective. If it is too much, I invite you to simply *observe* it. Do not judge, try to understand, change, fix, or get rid of it; instead, allow it to be as it is and it will pass by itself with time, and the understanding may reveal itself or not. Either is awesome. Respect where you are in your learning and journey and do not make yourself wrong if you don't get something. Consider it an adventure, not a destination; you will get there if you need to.

You may want to keep a journal to explore further what is coming up as you work through the exercises. Some exercises may be beneficial to repeat several times or can be used to work through specific issues to gain awareness. Keeping a journal can also help show your progress.

It can be easy to believe no progress is being made or that you are not getting anywhere. You may even think you are still working on the same belief or struggle or pattern; however, you may discover, if you look deeper, that you are approaching it from a different level or perspective, peeling back layers, and gaining new insight. Keeping a record may help you uncover your themes (the things you are here to learn and embody) as these are the ones that will come up again and again and be revisited to gain true wisdom and genius in your lifetime). These are things you are here to truly know, as part of your purpose. Keeping a journal helps keep a record of what is calling to be noticed.

Journals are an invaluable way to help work through issues. During challenging times, they can be used to document, process, and heal aspects of life. Once that area feels complete, burning the journal can help transmute the energy, creating a greater opportunity to transition to what is next.

Explore your relationship with yourself. Your ultimate aim may be to stop *trying* to be someone you are not, or someone that someone else wants you to be. Embrace and embody all of who you really are, warts, wrinkles, and all.

We may have been taught to live in the "real" world... however what is truly real is beyond our wildest imagination, and we may need to unlearn a lot of what we think we know as true. One of the first and most valuable lessons may be to reverse what you learned about having to have an explanation for everything. Enjoy your irrational, unreasonable, and wild self and *imagination*.

Please remember, you don't always have to be happy. You are also not doing something wrong if you are unhappy, or when bad things happen. Loss, tragedy, sadness, crisis, chaos, challenges, and struggles are all important aspects of life. A wave has crests and troughs. Without the ups and downs, life is a flat line. We cannot know happiness without sadness or light without dark.

Joy does not need a reason. Joy is independent of and sometimes even contradictory to what is happening around you. You can remain connected with your joy despite unhappy events. You can feel joy while concurrently feeling deep empathy or concern for another. By remaining connected with your joy, you can better assist others as the higher vibration of joy makes it possible to transmute pain and sorrow without saying or doing anything (higher frequency cancels out lower frequency). If someone is in quicksand, don't jump in with them. Stay on solid ground, hold a vision of joy for them, and offer a branch until they can grasp or accept it for themselves.

Are you ready to initiate a joyous adventure? Here is your first journaling or contemplation exercise. A few realigning questions:

- What does joy mean to you?
- When was the last time you felt joy?
- Where were you? What were you doing? What was happening?
- Do you know what causes joy to arise within you?

My Story

A bit about me in case you want to know who you are spending time with while reading, or if you'd like to know why I do what I do, how I came to be on this path, and whether I feel aligned for you.

Born the "black heifer" between two blonde sheep and measuring my worth by a scrapbook of cards sent after my birth (which was half the thickness and fullness of my siblings) did not assist in setting myself up to feel worthy and like I belonged.

Seen as too quiet, too shy, too sensitive, too tender, or too soft-hearted, along with being called stubborn, moody, cold hearted, and schizophrenic, did not help me at all. In fact, it served to isolate and confuse me. I didn't seem to work like everyone else. My energy levels were extreme. I bounced off the walls in one moment and was called lazy, unable to get up at all in the next.

Even though I wanted the experience of going to boarding school, I struggled to fit in. I also had permanent cold symptoms that only cleared between terms. Only in my forties upon discovering the extent of my empathic and sensitive nature did I understand why living among so many teenagers was so hugely challenging for me.

There were many times I wanted the world to stop, so I could hop off. I wanted out as things often felt too overwhelming or too harsh. I felt inadequate to deal with things. Interestingly, when the opportunity and "big screen of death" rolled down and played out my life, I found myself praying to God to help me stay. It was not me driving the tractor over the bridge that day, as I was fumbling around on the floor trying to unstick the accelerator with my hands.

The major health issues I experienced were related to energy, including chronic fatigue and burnout, three times in three different ways. In my twenties, it was physically; thirties, emotionally and mentally; late forties, in all ways with post-traumatic stress (PTS).

At university I was "legendary" for the amount of alcohol I could consume, and I was a happy drunk... until I wasn't. I experienced hyperactive episodes where I would actually run circles around my friends (like a sheepdog) because I could not physically slow down.

In my mid to late twenties, I was diagnosed with various syndromes and disorders (which must be medical speak for "we don't know what is wrong with you"). At one point, I had a strange neurological challenge where my legs would just suddenly stop working or freeze... usually when crossing a busy road. Halfway across, they would just stop walking, so there I would be staring down oncoming traffic, screaming in my head for my legs to move. When they did it was like running through treacle.

Food sensitivity was another thing. I struggled with dairy, wheat, gluten, sugar, yeasts, moulds, alcohol; you name it and I struggled with it. Throw in a few seizures and concussions and that really kept things interesting. Doctors were bewildered, throwing darts at tests and medications. Nothing felt aligned, so I looked for alternatives.

Traditional Chinese Medicine was my first success and worked amazingly for me. I used all the energy I had to drag myself to my appointment. After, I had to stop myself from running home.

My mid-thirties were full-on (undiagnosed) bipolar time, where days of euphoria were followed by weeks of depression, sometimes with suicidal tendencies. The higher the highs, the longer and deeper the lows. Using some socially acceptable addictions helped to keep me from my true feelings.

When I was "making it in the real world," I was managing multiple million-dollar projects for Y2K and trying to keep it all together. After living from pay cheque to pay cheque, my salary more than doubled in a day on a few occasions. The more the money rolled in, the more I rocked in the corner. When the outer world got "better," the inner world crumbled.

The nights alone with my emotions and thoughts were the worst. I was too tired and angry to cry and replayed every detail of the day over and over. Every conversation, every interaction—how should or could I have done it better? What should I have said or done? Making myself wrong and doubting myself at every turn while working as a female in a male-dominated industry meant working twice as hard to prove I was just as good (delivering projects they hadn't been able to). I put a lot of pressure on myself and wondered when the shoe would drop.

Then, the shoe dropped. Walking to the train, my shoe came off. It was only then that I noticed one was black and one was blue, *and* one was flat while the other one had an inch-and-a-half heel! I had just walked over two hundred metres from the car park. I broke down in tears and walked back in stockings to the car. I rang work and said, "I can't come in today. My shoes don't match."

My healer and saviour turned out to be a horse who *cracked* me open in many ways. Reconnecting with animals and nature helped me heal when nothing else made sense. I put my scientific and skeptical mind to work, exploring and experimenting with alternative and new age approaches. I found answers to my questions and questions to my answers.

I discovered the importance of emotions and connection with nature and spirit, which became my way of healing and realigning my health. I discovered how we can be energetically entangled with others and pets. My horse often got injured or sick when I was not tending to my emotions and thoughts or needed to be shown my misalignment. When I aligned them, my horse would get better. As I got healthier and happier, so did my pets and I got to take the vet off speed dial.

In my early forties, I followed my childhood passion to work with racehorses. I had not expected the horses would teach me so much about people, corporate systems, and energy, and I find I am still uncovering their teachings.

From my mid-thirties to fifty, I lived, breathed, studied, work-shopped, experienced, and experimented with every healing practice that interested me. Weaving common threads and patterns with the intent to find the most effective and simplest combinations, I found that essentially, simply being aware and present is the most powerful healing and realignment strategy. It was what the horses had been teaching me and showing me all along.

My third burnout was around fifty, which included a workplace injury and drawn-out insurance compensation claim via Work Cover which triggered and exacerbated PTS. The employer and insurer did little to consider or address trauma or PTS, so I researched it for myself. I was not expecting to also have my eyes opened to how many of the systems that were meant to support, protect, and make me better were in fact damaging, injuring, and making me worse. I realised the only way I was going to get better, was to take a leap of faith and get out of the system (resign from work and relinquish insurance payouts).

───────────〜───────────

I do not claim to be an expert, simply an adventurer and explorer of my inner world where there is still much to discover. The aim of this book is to share what has worked for me, which includes experiences, teachings, and knowledge that has become wisdom through living and embodying it.

Enjoy your adventure in disentangling from who you are not, discovering and finding peace within who you *are*, and realigning so joy can reconnect with you.

Part I

Realigning Joy

Joy and happiness are not different words for the same thing, despite what many dictionaries or thesauruses might say. So, what *is* the difference? Why joy and not just happiness?

Happiness is a reaction or an external expression based on emotions which arise from our thoughts.

Joy is an internal resonance or response that is independent of or does not react to emotional whims or thoughts.

Emotions come in waves, and like waves, we can ride them, surf them, or allow them to pass. Joy is an eternal internal resource.

Happiness is the wave.

Joy is the ocean.

Wind creates waves on the ocean. Similarly, thoughts create waves of emotions whipped up by internal and external events. Joy, like the ocean, always lies beneath the wave, yet when you are the boat in a storm, it is the waves that get your attention, more than the ocean.

If you have ever surfed, you will know the best way to work with an approaching wave is to face it and dive into or under it as it passes over. Similarly, when we face our emotions, if we dive in and feel them, then they will pass. We get smashed, slammed, or dumped when we attempt to avoid, deny, or escape the wave. Attempting to outrun or stop a wave is futile, whether the wave is oceanic or emotional.

Happiness depends on what is happening outside. It is psychological, like the thrill of the ride or chase and is easily impacted or lost by what is going on. It's like being happy and thrilled on the best wave ever, then suddenly being dumped and no longer happy or thrilled.

However, joy arises from within. It is spiritual, independent of external circumstances. It is internally generated and irrelevant to what is, or is not, happening around you. You can feel a sense of joy, even when external situations are sad. Being dumped by a wave (or wiped out) does not affect your joy. You maintain the thrill of being alive in the experience (of the ocean) despite changes in conditions.

Somebody or something can make you happy; however, nobody and nothing can make you joyous. Joy simply is... *or is not.*

We can pretend to be happy, but we cannot activate, force, or pretend to be joyous. We cannot work on joy directly; however, we may increase the possibility or probability of joy arising, by working on our happiness. The happier we feel and the more often we feel happy, the more likely we are to open ourselves to feeling joy, by removing the barriers that may not be allowing joy to float up to the surface.

Choose Joy

Although happiness is fleeting, as you can quickly shift *out* of happiness, you can also consciously shift *into* happiness by doing small things that make you happy.

Smiling, even when you do not feel like it, can lift your mood. With happiness, you may be able to fake it till you make it. However, it is really more nuanced than that. It is more about allowing the possibility to shift your bias towards happiness and less about overriding how you are feeling. It is like choosing to allow a smile to come even though you feel sad, rather than attempting or forcing a smile to override or change sadness (although this too can work and may be helpful in situations where you must get on with things). Give yourself a moment, to feel the difference between these two methods.

Allowing yourself to feel and give time to process the emotions you are feeling, such as sadness, is the most natural and powerful way to move emotions, as this process allows the emotional wave to move through and out of the body. Crying very often will naturally progress into laughter if we allow ourselves to ride the wave all the way in and all the way out.

A little aside about smiling: Share your smiles with others.

If you see someone who does not have one, gift them one of yours.

It's simply powerful. Lives can be changed and saved with a radiant I-see-you smile.

I know mine has.

The greatest power humans have is choice: choosing to find the gift in adversity and challenge, choosing to find light in the dark corners, choosing to see love in unsmiling faces, choosing to be willing to be joyful, choosing to stay true to yourself and your joy regardless of outside circumstances.

Making the choice, being willing, and asking the loving source that is within us all to bring more happiness and joy may be as difficult as it gets. We have been told, "Life is not meant to be easy." But why not? Whether you believe it or not, life can be, at the very least, a bit easier.

What Does God Mean to You?

Joy, although felt or experienced through our physical, mental, and emotional bodies, is sourced via the spiritual body, so it is difficult to speak of joy without speaking of spirit or God. Although you do not need to believe in God to feel joy, it is a state of unified connection to something greater than you or us (which may be called God or any variety of names) and why an open discussion on the concept of God may be relevant here. I share my perceptions and experiences to provide the angle from which I have written this book and to maybe invite you into thinking about what God means to you.

In addressing my interpretation of God, know that I honour and respect your own personal experiences, meanings, and perceptions of God and what God means to you. I do not wish to change your belief, convert you, or convince you differently, so please feel free to skip this section. Just know before you go that there are a number of words or terms I use interchangeably, in reference to what is more universally known as God, such as The Universe, Source, The Force, Universal Law, The Divine, All That Is, Prime Creator, Unity Consciousness, and variations of these. The qualities of unconditional love, joy, grace, forgiveness, and peace are used to describe how we feel when connected with this God source.

I used to be very triggered by the word *God* and for some time refused to say it or even acknowledge there might be a God, so if the word *God* is triggering or loaded for you, I invite you to simply replace it with your name for whatever you call God. I acknowledge that *God*, *religion*, or the *concept of God* is very personal; this is just my perspective with no intention to convert or debate.

The God that religion told me about, did not feel like the one I felt I knew. The sermons of sin, hell, and threats of God's vengeance and anger did not feel aligned. The image of the crucifixion did not feel like an empowering, nurturing, or loving symbol, but my teachers were adults, and this rhetoric had been taught for ages. I was only a child; what did I know?

From religious teachings, I felt betrayed and hated God for all the suffering he was causing, so I stopped talking with Him. Sermons of damnation and images of Jesus on the cross caused me to misalign with religion. I wondered why they kept telling these stories, as they did not make me want to love others more or be a better person; instead, they made me want to dislike and distrust people.

Through experience and research, I learned to distinguish the God of religion and the God of spirituality, and in time, I rekindled our relationship. My impression of and relationship with God has changed largely thanks to the spiritual teachings of:

- Neale Donald Walsch's *Conversations with God* because he talked with God the way I did… and for which I had previously been making myself wrong.

- Caroline Myss's spiritual teachings and prayers both touched and resonated with me because of her practical and reverent understanding and knowledge of spiritual texts, history, religion, and Mysticism.

- Helen Schucman's *A Course in Miracles* from which two things really stood out for me: fear is the absence of love, and we have been focusing on the crucifixion (fear) rather than the resurrection (love).

I often wonder how different my experience and perspective of life would have been if right from the beginning, instead of being drowned in sin, fear, and images of suffering and crucifixion, I was instead swimming in the joy, love, and celebration of eternal life and images of resurrection. How different would our lives be if we were immersed not in fear and death, but in the joy of life and living?

My less skeptical perception of God has been founded more thoroughly where science and religion meet—Quantum Science.

Religion says, "God is in all things," "God is everywhere," and "God is Love," and science says, "Everything is Energy."

Energy is God and God is Energy. And the energy said to hold everything together is love, which brings us full circle: God is love or consciousness. Or the many names given by science, such as space, energy, law or "the field." It may be worth noting God can be many things, and just as our perception of God has been distorted, so too has our perception of love and what it truly is.

I see God or Creative Source as the space between matter that holds everything together—the space between stars, atoms, quarks, and leptons (and anything smaller we have not discovered). I feel God or Source as the stillness between breaths and as the laws and forces that govern The Universe and keep everything in alignment and in divine order. I see God as The Universe, the body that contains galaxies, planets, and stars; just like our body contains organs and cells. I see God as love and its whole spectrum; as Divine Light—the energy of light and information; as the life force energy that exists in all matter and all things. I see God as All That Is and all that can be or is to be. Ultimately, I believe God is many things and does not care what we call him/her/it/them as God contains all pronouns.

How I came to make sense of the terrible things that happen is that God is not vengeful, angry, or punishing, but is a loving presence and source that allows free will to operate within Universal Laws here on Earth. God makes no judgements of good or bad and does not interfere or intervene *unless we ask* (which is what prayer is). We come to Earth to learn or have experiences and sometimes this is through bad things. Our greatest adversaries may in fact, be our most beloved friends in another reality, who agreed to help us with the experiences and lessons we came to have. So even though things may appear outwardly bad, good things are also happening.

It is human to judge good and bad, right and wrong. It is human to assign meaning, to label, and to separate—but that's not God's way. Everything is neutral; nothing is personal, although it is very intimate.

What Are Emotions?

Emotions are energy in motion (e-Motion) or waves of energy that trigger chemical signals or messengers in our body that we can feel.

Our emotions are not actually "ours." They are received and transmitted like radio or television waves and we pick up what is "on the airwaves." If we are "tuned in" or if it resonates with us, we will pick it up, similar to how another tuning fork will vibrate if another of the same frequency is struck. The vibrations trigger chemical responses that we feel in the body as emotions.

This is how I have come to understand and work with emotional energy, which may be very different from what you may have been taught or understood. So, bear with me (and trust your intuition as to whether this feels aligned for you) and follow me through this string if you are up for a bit of quantum science... here we go:

  ➢ Science says, "Everything is energy."
  ➢ Religion says, "God is everything."
  ➢ Spirituality says, "Consciousness is everything."

And

  ➢ Emotions are energy in motion (e-Motion).
  ➢ Emotions are chemical messengers (biofeedback) that respond with, and to, our environment and thoughts and help us navigate our environment.

- Thought adds meaning to emotional messages (and can entangle us).

If God is everything, God is everywhere, and everything is energy, then having emotions (energy in motion) is one of the ways in which we receive guidance from our environment and communicate with God. (Note that when I mention *environment*, it is in the broadest context of all things that influence or impact us externally and internally and is not just limited to the natural world).

Now in relation to healing and aligning.

Science says:

- Energy can neither be created nor destroyed but can be transformed from one state to another.
- Energy can be either a particle or a wave.
- Whether it is a particle or a wave depends on the observer.
- YOU are the observer!
- The emotional wave has been measured to last on average around ninety seconds.

Why is this relevant or important?

- An emotional wave is energy and data (a message from The Universe, another, or environment).
- When an emotional wave is stopped in your body (such as when you do not allow yourself to feel the emotional wave all the way through, or you supress, reject, deny, or react to the emotion), you can stop the message.
- When you do not allow the message to be delivered or do not receive the full message the emotion (wave) collapses into a particle and creates matter (the matter is concreted or unresolved).
- Matter becomes located, i.e., the particle gets lodged or stuck in your body.

- Additional emotional waves may also be stopped, adding to the backlog and entanglement—the more energy is trapped, the more pain can result.
- Energy wants to move.
- If trapped or unable to move, heat is created.
- Heat can cause discomfort and pain (also called inflame-mation).
- Pain is an escalating alarm for a pending message that needs to be received or read.
- If the message (or pain) is left unattended or is not *observed*, more pain, dis-comfort, or dis-ease may result.
- If we are able to *observe* (notice, acknowledge, and accept) the (now painful) message, the particle (through being observed) can return to a wave.
- The wave can wave goodbye to you and (hopefully) you can wave goodbye to pain!

If we can be present for about a minute and a half (with the gift of energy and information these emotions are presenting) at the time of delivery, the wave will not collapse into a particle, as it can be observed as the message or energy received, and the wave can keep moving through. This is why it is vital to be present or *in the now*, which translates to being a witness to what is and how we may simply observe without reacting or adding energy or meaning by analysing, defending, resisting, or fighting it.

Trapped emotions can be located by where we feel pain or dis-comfort in the body. By being present with and observing the emotions for as long as it takes to create a shift, we can change the particle back into a wave, allowing it to flow naturally out of our bodies.

It is never too late to observe the emotion and its message; in fact, pain is saying, "You are here!" frozen in body, space, and time. Its location provides a lot of information of what it is about (as it settles where there is resonance).

Hips are a storehouse of trapped emotional energy and represent balance (physically and figuratively). When we do not maintain emotional balance, or we "sit" on our emotions, it gets stored in the hips and pelvic area. A lifetime of suppressed emotions and emotional energy may result in hip problems in later life and may be one of the overlooked and underlying reasons for hip replacements.

There is one last point that creates distinction between emotions (happiness) and states (joy). In addition to the four elements (fire, earth, air, water) there is also a fifth—ether (or spirit). Science does not generally acknowledge ether's existence (except as a constant or force to make a few equations work). Science has a questionable practice of denying the existence of that which cannot be measured, explained, or its function determined (and is why science says 98 percent of human DNA is junk).

I believe the element ether helps explain the difference between emotions (happiness) and states (joy). Where emotions are fleeting waves of energy, ether is a constant force that infuses and pervades all things. Like wind and other events create waves on the ocean, events and happenings create waves on the ocean of All That Is, and we call them emotions.

Realigning Exercise:
Moving Emotional Energy

Simple presence in allowing yourself to feel what you are feeling is profoundly powerful, as it activates the *observer*.

Being observed by another, in the sense of having your feelings witnessed, is profoundly and miraculously transformative, helping move, transition, heal, and align emotions with great ease.

If you consider emotions simply as "flavours" of life that add to your wonder (not just your challenges), or if you consider emotions as your connection with yourself and your intuition, do you feel that you would be happier and more aligned to receive their messages?

Simple practice:

Is there something that even just thinking about, makes you become emotionally charged (such as angry, frustrated, disappointed, or bitter)?

It can be personal or more general (e.g., politics, inequality, environment).

Before you begin, please remember the power of breath. Breath is a powerful way to shift energy, so if things get a bit heated or uncomfortable, focus on your breath or breathe through it by directing your breath to where you are feeling (or not feeling) the energy.

1. While thinking about this situation, observe or notice what you are feeling. Do your best to simply allow it to be as it is—do not be tempted to judge, criticise, assess, debate, analyse, change, or fix—observe it objectively and neutrally from a distance. *Observe* thoughts and energy, without engaging.

2. Become aware of the sensations in your body and any thoughts or pain. You may acknowledge this by stating, "I feel _____" such as, "I feel pain and discomfort in my back," or "I feel anxious and sick to my stomach about doing this speech," or "I feel overwhelmed/frozen/numb,"

or even "I don't know how or what I am feeling, but it doesn't feel good."

3. Just sit with it for at least two to three minutes, accepting what you are or are not feeling. As it is. Allowing and accepting what you are feeling (or not feeling) to be that way. If it gets uncomfortable, simply breathe.

4. After a while, if you are able to remain truly observant, you will feel a shift.

5. If you are having difficulty, ask yourself, "Am I willing to feel how I feel in this present moment of time?" Simply sit and allow (observe) that willingness or unwillingness to be there. Information may arise or it might not—either is good.

Stay with that feeling. If it moves to another location in your body, simply follow and observe until it naturally resolves, fades, dissolves, shifts… or does whatever it does (as the emotional particle changes into a wave and moves out of your body).

Please note, the pain may not go completely or go immediately away. This may take several goes as it may be multilayered. A shift or movement of any kind is progress. It may feel more intense, although it does not need to, in order to create profound and deep realignment. Things can simply fade.

For more complex issues, you may need a bit more:

1. Notice and observe in your body where you feel pain or discomfort.

2. Acknowledge how or what you are feeling. It may help to say, "I feel pain in <location> and it feels like <sensation>." Be willing to simply allow it to be without attempting to change, fix, move, or do anything. Simply feel it.

3. You may ask, "Do you have a message for me?" and do your best to accept this message without prejudice, judgement, criticism, blame, shame, or guilt. If any of these do

arise, accept that they are there (no use feeling guilty about feeling guilty).

4. Check "Do I need to forgive anyone or anything?" then "Where do I need to forgive myself?" (Do not skip this step; this is where transformation really happens).

5. Ask "How could I perceive or imagine this in a more empowering way?" or "How would *love* see or express this?"

6. Ask "What is one step I can take right now to support this change?"

This may seem to be a very simple exercise and it is; however, it can be profoundly healing if you can remember to work with and through your emotions in the moment they are happening. Allow their message to be delivered and received (whether you get the message consciously or not) and sit with it until you feel a shift of clearing of energy. You may discover that you have greater movement and freedom within the body, which allows joy to move within you, not just through you.

Crying

When we think of emotions, it doesn't take long to associate emotions with crying. What we may not realise is how vitally important crying is to our health and well-being. When we stop ourselves or others from crying, we stop a self-healing and alchemising process.

Tears and crying have a healing effect on the body. When we cry, we release oxytocin and endorphins (feel good hormones), and it helps the nervous system to rest and relax.

Many ways of parenting that have been passed down or taught, especially in regards to crying, have been a little dysfunctional at best, but please do not blame your parents, or yourself if you are a parent, as parents *always* do the best they can with the resources and knowledge they have at the time in that moment (and that may change from moment to moment depending on what is going on).

Crying is how a baby communicates they have needs to be met, such as hunger, thirst, or changing. It is not commonly recognised that at certain times crying *is* their need. It is *not* about crying alone or just being *observed*, it is being able to cry uninhibited in the loving arms or presence of an emotionally regulated adult. This practice can heal birth trauma and help discharge emotional and sensory overwhelm from the day's experiences, which assists a baby to relax and sleep.

Aware Parenting teaches how many techniques used to stop crying (such as dummies, pacifiers, rocking, and jiggling) can create dissociative or distracted behaviours. If a baby's innate ability to heal, realign, or regulate their nervous system is not fully engaged (through crying) their ability to be in direct connection with joy is inhibited.

The initial reaction or response for many parents with a crying baby is to stop them crying as quickly as possible or leave them to cry alone, unaware of the healing effects of simply allowing (with loving presence) time for the emotional wave to pass all the way through. The emotional intelligence of parents is vital, as children pick up on their distress and emotions. When babies are full, tired, or overwhelmed, they cry.

When we block tears, we also turn off the rest and digest part (yes, we "digest" emotions too) of the nervous system and activate the fight-or-flight parts of the nervous system, resulting in becoming more stressed.

Crying is one way we process emotions and release tension. How much better do you feel after a good cry, especially after a stressful or traumatic event? You actually do wash away stress with tears, as crying is a natural release of overwhelming and stored emotional energy.

For many years I could not cry for myself. People would do and say awful things, but I would not cry. Yet, if someone did or said that to another, I would cry for *them*. Today I cry often for sadness and also for joy. I wish I could say it feels comfortable; however, in many situations it does not, more due to the discomfort of others.

When it is just me, or when I am with others who are comfortable with the emotional release called crying, I can feel the freedom and invitation to cry openly and unapologetically.

It feels amazing to be able to cry and be messy in the presence of another, knowing you are supported and not judged. To feel the resonance of another who can hold space with you while you cry is truly healing and cathartic.

It can be more challenging to cry in public and especially when others get distressed or uncomfortable around crying.

If there is one favour that we can do for ourselves and others, it is to get more comfortable with crying and tears and to allow and welcome tears. We would be a happier and healthier society if we were allowed and encouraged to cry, rather than told (directly or indirectly) to stuff down (and keep down) all that emotional energy.

We have been so disempowered, blocked, and hindered from our beautiful expressions of ourselves and how we are feeling by not being allowed to cry. Boys have a lot to cry about. Girls have a lot to be angry about. We have not been allowed to feel what we feel.

There is only so much that can be pushed down, swallowed, suppressed, invalidated, sucked up, or stiff upper lipped. The tears that want to come out must go somewhere and the jar can only get so full before the lid has to come off. And when it does, it often comes off in explosive, violent, reactive, and destructive ways. I believe much of the violence we see today is suppressed emotional energy bursting out and no longer able to be contained.

Apparently, in some tribes the inability for someone to cry is considered a potential threat to the safety of the tribe, which is a very different response from Western culture, where lack of tears is worn like a badge of honour.

What a different world it would be if we had been taught and allowed right from the start to embody this very powerful and creative emotional energy. Start today with allowing yourself to cry when you need to and feel safe to. You may not feel it right away; however, a reverberation from crying is often a sense of peace or quiet joy.

Realigning Exercise:
Have a Good Cry

Next time when you have the reason *and* the space, capacity, and safety to cry undisturbed, could you allow yourself to really cry?

Could you allow yourself to get this messy?

- Tears rolling all the way down your face, dripping off your chin, running down your chest or between your breasts right into your navel.
- Blowing snot bubbles.
- Being unable to string your words together, only able to speak in punctuated— single – words – spaced – between—gasps.
- Drinking your own tears.
- Blubbering, howling, or making the noises needed to express how you feel.
- Really surrendering to the cry and allowing yourself to let out and let go of stored emotional energy seeking a way out.
- Crying for what invoked you to cry now.
- Crying for what has happened in the past, or what you anticipate in the future.
- Crying tears for what has been held back, pushed down, sucked up, or wiped away too soon.

Tears are healing and transformative, which is why we feel better after a good cry. When you stop, wipe, or brush your tears away, you also brush away and stop the transformative healing process through the chemicals, the cleansing and soothing processes that tears and crying produce.

Do you, or could you, allow yourself to really cry and be messy to receive the full benefits and healing it provides?

If you need a *reason* to cry or to help you get started, watch a movie, documentary, or story that you know will help you access your tears. Set yourself up with a box of tissues and see how long you can delay using them.

Messy with snot bubbles is what you are going for. As you clear and release the sad, you make more room for joy to occupy.

Love and Joy Are Not Emotions

Your best defence in this world is love and joy, as nothing can penetrate them because there is no opposite. Love and joy are either present or not. Love and joy are life forces, not emotion. What does this mean exactly, though?

Love is not sentiment, nor is it the romanticised emotion we commonly associate with Hollywood movies and romcoms. Similarly, joy, grief, forgiveness, and peace are not emotions either; they are aspects or expressions of the state of love and the depth to which we feel it. Joy is a state we feel when we are in love, grief when we feel the loss of that love, forgiveness is love's transmutative power, and peace is what we feel when we are at one with love. It is the feedback received when connected and aligned to ourselves and to our *life force* that can be felt totally and that reverberates throughout our bodies.

Love, joy, grief, forgiveness, truth, and peace can remain intact regardless of what is going on and regardless of other emotions being felt. You can feel happy while grieving or feel sad even though you are joyous.

Generally, we mash all feelings into one without distinguishing states of being (love, joy, grief) from emotions (lust, happiness, sadness); we just consider them all one and the same. Emotions such as happiness, sadness, shame, anger, fear, surprise, and disgust are, by nature, fleeting, changeable, and unreliable. Emotions are chemical feedback, showing us how we relate to our environment and the world around us, and we can feel different about the same things at different times.

We do not always (and will not always) feel the same way or have the same emotional reaction to the same events or things. Our emotional reactions change when we change what those events or things mean to us. What used to trigger anger will fail to once we have realigned understanding and forgiveness of said event, situation, or person.

Emotion (e-Motion) is energy in motion, and thus is not really *your own* emotional energy. Emotional waves are all around you, like radio waves, where you can tune in to "pick them up." In this way you can also pick up the emotional energy waves of others—yet feel and act as if it is yours. Have you ever found yourself in a surprisingly bad mood all of a sudden for no particular reason? Had you passed an angry person on the street, walked into a room after a fight or witnessed others fighting? This is one way we can take on others' emotional energy.

We get entangled when we take emotions personally, thinking or believing that it is who we are or that they are *ours* to take home—like a lost puppy dog. Although we have a very important and intimate relationship with emotions, they're best not to keep—as like the puppy dog, it is probably someone else's to take care of.

Remember emotions are simply biochemical feedback, a mechanism for communicating and navigating the world by how we feel.

Realigning Exercise:
I Am Not "My" Emotions

This realigning exercise is to help you feel the difference a few words can make.

When you say "I am" you are invoking great spiritual forces and thus need to be mindful and careful what words you attach with it, as it creates powerful affirmations.

When you say you are your emotions, you can severely limit and disempower yourself. In order to not undermine your power and who you really are consider this.

Instead of saying:

> "I am _____ (angry, sad, happy…)"

Say:

> "I am *feeling* _____ (angry, sad, happy…)"

Don't believe one word could make a difference?

Take a deep breath and put your hand on your heart.

Say "I am sad" out loud and notice:

- Where do you feel it in your body?
- How does it feel?
- Out of a score of 0-10 with 10 feeling good or energised, how do you feel?

Say "I am feeling sad" out loud.

- Where do you feel it in your body?
- Does it feel different?
- How or where does it feel different?
- Out of a score of 0-10 with 10 feeling good or energised, how do you feel?

Feel into how taking it a step further impacts you by making it less identified by removing "I am," by switching out to a less personalised level, so that:

My or *I* is swapped out for *this* or *the*. So, "My sadness is heavy" or "I am feeling sad and heavy" becomes *this* or *the*, such as "THE sadness is heavy" or "THIS sadness feels heavy."

Watch for the distinction of where you own something and where it owns you.

Unapologetically Take Your Place

Now that you have a connection with the power of words, it is time to create a different story and a more empowering narrative for your life.

We are each like a piece of a jigsaw. When we do not take our rightful place, our absence is felt deeply and noticed by the whole. The picture is incomplete.

When we follow the status quo, imitate others, or allow others to tell us what we are, how we are, or who we should be, we may not fit or fill our rightful place. When we allow fear to stop us from expressing ourselves fully, or when we are not being who we truly know ourselves to be, we leave a me-shaped hole.

Equally, when we try to force or jam ourselves into a position we were not meant to occupy, it never feels like a good fit. We never truly feel the satisfaction of being home and feeling *at* home. Instead, we may feel like we do not belong, a bit off colour, or mismatched for our surroundings. The picture is altered; it does not feel whole or have integrity—and neither do we.

Your very existence is important. Take your place and allow yourself to feel, express, and share the joy that comes with being the person that *you* are and enjoy being who you are in the right place, at the right time, as you feel snug in the perfect fit. If you do not feel you are in your place, please know that you are exactly where you are meant to be right now. You may not feel secure in your place yet as the other pieces surrounding you may not yet be in place, or you may still be finding your way to your spot. To achieve a snug fit, all surrounding pieces need to be in their places also. When aligned, you are also magnetic and more likely to attract the pieces you need to surround and support you.

Our unique self is being *part of* the whole, taking our *individual place within the whole* matrix. We must take care of ourselves so we can take care of others. We must also be true to ourselves because it allows and gives permission for others to be true to themselves. We become self-*full*, not self-*less*.

We need others and others need us. We are not meant to do the entire journey alone. Through our relationships we get to know ourselves. Everything we do, or do not do, touches others. We are all swimming in the same ocean and our actions create waves that ripple out. There is a profound truth: when you live and do what is truly aligned for you, you *also* do what is aligned for others.

We are in this together and "to-get-her(e)" we need you to be your intuitive, brilliant, awesome, miraculous, amazing, genius-aligned self, right here, right now. The world needs you to be you, not someone else—that spot is already taken.

Change Is Life's Dance

Change is not something that only impacts you; it sends out a ripple and we may not make the changes we would like, due to how it may impact others. Change is one of the few guarantees in life, and sometimes if we do not dance, the dance comes to us. Change is movement, and life is the dance.

Change can be daunting and scary; however, could it be less so if we were to approach it as a dance, knowing that when we dance, it gives others permission to dance too?

When you take or make different steps, it changes the dance. A good dance partner will come to meet you, flowing with and intuiting the new steps, maybe adding a few of their own for finesse. There may initially be a stage of chaos before the rhythm is found and things fall back in step and synchronicity. There is choice in a dance—choice to flow or resist, choice to lead or follow, choice to stay and learn new steps, choice to stop the dance, and choice to leave, or return, to the dance floor.

Making change in even just one aspect of your life will naturally flow into other aspects of your life. How you do one thing is how you do all things—it is the dance. When you improve your relationship with yourself (by being who or how you need to be right now), improvement will also naturally flow into your relationships with others, and also with money, health, and work as it changes the way you dance and the way you energetically relate with them.

When things get to be too much (and they will at times), it is a sign to give yourself space and time to allow your nervous system to catch up. You may need to catch your breath or reset your frame and rhythm. Sometimes you need to make up the steps as you go along. Have fun; find your own beat and rhythm.

Life's challenges and adventures all have the higher perspective of realigning us with who we truly are and to connect us with our dance. A dance step backwards or sideways is not positive or negative, good or bad, right or wrong; each step *is* the dance.

In life, an accident or illness can be seen as one of the more technical challenges or lifts in a routine. You may fall to the floor many times while learning and developing strength, but if you continue to face it and transmute it—it can launch you joyfully into a wonderful dance connected with direction and purpose.

Your dance may not be seen as graceful; however, it is grace filled. There are many ways to align, and some can be profoundly mysterious and deeply confusing until understood for what they are. Allow confusion to simply be there—dance it out, rather than getting entangled in the confusion.

Embrace change and enjoy your dance with The Universe.

Part II

Realigning Self

We constantly go in and come out of alignment, as we are constantly realigning. This is not because you are doing something wrong; it is simply how harmony, homeostasis, and balance works. Life and you move in and through waves, which have peaks and troughs. Life is *not* a flat line—death is. When we fall way out of alignment, it is due to greater extremes in waves, which may require more conscious input, action, or change to realign.

In this chapter we will discuss conditioning and its many forms. Conditioning is one of the main ways we become less like ourselves and thus out of alignment with who we really are. We will also look at the power of words and stories and how they can misalign or realign our lives.

There are generally two ways in which we can initiate change or realign. We can make small changes over a long time or make big changes over a short time.

Big changes can have a dramatic impact and can change our lives for better (although they may feel like *for worse* at the time). Big changes may be what is called the dark night of the soul, where we face darker, unwanted, or uncomfortable aspects. This may happen through experiences such as accidents, illness, and shocks or through miraculous, gracious, and fortunate occurrences.

Shocks and accidents can make us reassess our lives and be catalysts for making changes that need to be made to align with the healthier, more joyous version of ourselves.

Dark night of the soul experiences vary greatly in impact and duration; however, they share a common theme. They are the experiences often building over months or years that bring us to our knees, and when we hit rock bottom, when we feel that we have nothing left to give, no fight left... we surrender (too exhausted to resist or fight our self-induced fears and limitations any longer). When we realise the only thing we are fighting against is our ego, and the moment we stop allowing the ego to run the show, our soul shines through. The soul penetrates through the cracks and lights up the darkness.

I have had many dark nights of the soul; some lasting for years. The physical dark night when I felt like my body was betraying me (as there was no way that the alcohol, cigarettes, junk food, parties, late nights, and shift work could be the problem!), I would make some changes; one thing would get better and then more would go wrong and things got worse. It felt like one thing after the other and like it would never end. One night I was in so much physical and emotional pain I yelled out (to nobody in particular), "Come on. Give me your worst." I surrendered to it and after a while, the pain subsided. This reprieve began the recovery process and helped me seek, receive, and accept the help I needed to continue getting better.

The mental-emotional dark night was due to an obsessive mind, which I will call *IT* as IT did not feel all mine or like I had control over it, and I was stressed managing information technology (IT) projects at the time for Y2K. IT would replay the things that were or were not happening in the projects, what I had or had not done, what was not working, what was working and what could work better. I would run over problems in my mind, seeking solutions, which only came once I fell asleep... yet I was unable to sleep to get to the solution I needed.

IT fed my social anxiety and my feelings of not being good enough by amplifying and replaying conversations over and over again. *Why did I say that? Why did I say it like that? What was I thinking? What must they think? What will they say to others? When they looked at me, what did that mean? Why did I smile so weird? Why was I so stupid? Why didn't I say this? Why did I <insert denigrating comment here>?* On and on it went. Replaying, judging, and critiquing my day in a never-ending loop.

I was on adrenal overload, driving myself insane. I wanted to knock myself out just to get IT to shut up. I was depressed with suicidal thoughts, yet too concerned about how my suicide might impact others. I lay awake obsessed and too exhausted to sleep.

One very dark night, I managed to worry myself sick and was so completely exhausted, IT surrendered. For the first time in a very, very long time IT was quiet and peaceful. I fell asleep and slept the whole night *and* the whole next day, looking at the time and wondering why it was dark at 9 a.m. (it was 9 p.m.). It is not to say that during these dark periods I did not experience joy; however, it was short lived and after I resigned from my job, I found relief and joy that was more enduring.

Where dark nights can be considered big changes, there are also the small actions we take in everyday moments, which can either align or misalign us from our purpose and who we really are.

The small changes are the little things we do every day: the habits, routines, and seemingly insignificant things we do (for worse or better) that truly impact our lives. So how do you tell whether your routine or habits are healthy or not?

- Do you feel sustainably energised, revitalised, or satisfied?
- Do you feel good for extended periods after (rather than a high which crashes shortly after)?
- Are you truly present and connected with what you are doing?

The Wobbly or Squeaky Wheel

Some small things may dictate what bigger changes may be needed, like a seemingly insignificant wobbly or squeaky wheel, which does not stop us from getting where we want, yet does change the effort, ease, and comfort in which we arrive.

Small habits, addictions, obsessions, and strategies you use to avoid, disconnect, or numb how you are feeling can impact you in less desirable ways. Habits that are consuming (in both meanings) include behaviours such as drinking, smoking, and bingeing (television, food, social media, gaming, or other dis-tractions). However, healthy habits or routines such as exercise, work, and eating healthy can also become misaligned if they are obsessive, or used in a way to avoid, or distract you from your emotions or things that need to be addressed or from moving forward in your life.

Whether your misaligned wheel is insignificant or not, depends on how it influences, directs, or hijacks your choices.

- Does it stop you from doing something else?
- Does it consume your thoughts?
- Do you feel guilty or ashamed if or when you are not doing it?
- Does it stop you from feeling how you are feeling?
- Does it interfere with your relationship with others or yourself?
- Are your choices influenced or dictated by whether you can still do it or not?

Answering yes to any of these may mean your wheels need attention.

The wobble or squeak is an invitation to notice. The seemingly insignificant yet persistent niggle invites the opportunity to notice what needs realignment, and the squeak is a warning that it requires soothing.

We can attend to the niggles, or like so many of us do, wait until the wheels fall off or seize. The old *don't fix it until its broken* adage is not necessarily wrong as sometimes, we need to fully experience misalignment to make the big changes. The issue may come if we do not learn from these experiences and learn to realign earlier. Sometimes we need to know the consequences and the awareness that come from experience and the wisdom of hindsight.

Finding what you need to align can feel like shopping in a new, huge supermarket. It helps to have an intention (list) to keep focused. Sometimes you push your trolley up and down aisle after aisle before you find what you want and sometimes you get lucky and find it right away. Once you know where things are, you can go straight there.

So… what misaligns us and causes our wheels to wobble and squeak? Why do we often not feel free to be who we truly are? Short answer? *Conditioning!*

Realigning Exercise:
How Do You Shop?

Your stories and conditioning can drive unconscious or emotional choices that may not be truly aligned with you or for you. So, taking this shopping analogy further, it can be used to show you what you are navigating and how you are relating to life experiences. As in life, everything means everything and also means nothing. Life is navigating which is which.

Working with the shopping analogy as a broadened perspective or story, you can discover a lot about where things are misaligned in your life or where or how you need realignment. Remember, when approaching your inquiry, do so with curiosity and playfulness. It is not an exercise in beating yourself up, simply an opportunity to have fun (maybe even a chuckle) discovering more about your story.

For example, if you have a tendency to overfill or over shop:

- Is there a hole you are attempting to fill in your life with things?
- Do you feel there is something you need to overcompensate for?
- If overfilling bags, are you feeling stretched, overloaded, or ready to snap, or are you having trouble keeping a handle on things?

Look at what are you filling your cart with. Does it have a story in itself? If you're loading up with sweet treats:

- How can you reconnect with the sweetness of life (rather than things or sugar)?
- How can you treat yourself with more sweetness and kindness? (I.e., sourcing it internally rather than externally.)

Look at the imagery and story and be whimsical, as in any situation you may be able to ask:

- How does it apply to what is going on in my life?
- What message is it literally and figuratively showing me?
- What story can I make up from this? (It might be truer than fiction.)

What Is Conditioning?

Conditioning is the ways in which we get programmed. The beliefs, lessons, habits, and ways that get established over time through or by our parents, family, teachers, peers, work, society, culture, religion, news, media, social media, and advertising (you name it) that influence the way in which we operate in the world and the meaning we give things.

Conditioning can lead you to make choices and decisions that are not aligned with or best for you. Conditioning is at the foundation and is the cause of choices (good and bad) made by default or habit. Conditioning is present when you sabotage, say "should" or "have to," or make choices or decisions to please others.

We are now heading back to the supermarket, as it is a wonderful example of how we get conditioned without realising it. Supermarkets condition us and influence our choices, not just through advertising but also by use of specific lighting, colours, sounds, smells, and the big one—product placement. Which shelf, at what height, and where an item is located and placed in the store are intentional and based on research. Companies are willing to pay for placement, as it is so effective on our psychology.

Frequently bought everyday items, such as milk, are placed at the back of the store, so you have to walk all the way through the store to get to them, making it more likely that you will see and grab other items as you go. You may have come in just for milk, yet you are unlikely to leave with just that item, as you have to resist a lot of products screaming and pleading "buy me." If you did happen to successfully run the gauntlet and booby trapped aisles, full of "shelf talkers" (cards with sales, special prices, and product descriptions) in aisles and end pop-up displays or demonstrations that get in your way or in your face... and you had resisted all temptations..., you now find yourself standing in front of the biggest challenge, the final assault before you are free: the sweet snacks and sugar-loaded treats at the checkout!

Everything in a supermarket is carefully orchestrated, organised, and designed to condition or influence your behaviour (buy more) and is designed to coerce you into making certain choices (buy more), to make choices you might not otherwise make (and buy more). Even if you were fully conscious and aligned within yourself, it can still be difficult as, in all honesty, they have it down to a fine art. Even with awareness it is easy to fall into the trap (and buy more). Did you realise the supermarket is such a psychological minefield?

Sadly, it doesn't stop there. We eat these intentionally designed addictive food items and dislike ourselves for it (thinking we should be strong enough to resist). We lower our opinion of ourselves, feel bad or guilty, and lower our energetic frequency, all making us more likely to do it all again (and buy more).

Everything on the shelf is vying for our attention, and it is more often our conditioned (or hijacked) self that makes the purchases, rather than our aligned, fully conscious self.

- Have you ever stopped to question why you actually buy or choose the products and brands you do?
- Do you get hijacked by sale items and buy things you do not really need?
- Was that bargain really a bargain?
- Do you honestly need that much toilet paper?
- What drives you to buy what you do?
- Are you aware of how you are being conditioned?

Conditioning is why you get home and wonder why you bought half of what you did. Conditioning is why you get everything *except* what you went in for as you lose your rational self.

Just as it can be difficult to walk into a supermarket and not be influenced by its conditioning field, so too in our lives, it can be very difficult to only get what we need or only get what is on our list. We live in a conditioning field. Our own bodies are a conditioned field, as our genetic code is conditioned by our ancestors' experiences which influence our reactions and behaviours.

Being influenced by and responding to conditioning isn't about fault and is not something to be ashamed for or to make yourself wrong about. Knowledge is power, and if you know where you are most vulnerable to being conditioned, you can take steps to be less impacted. Although I can say from experience, you can take all the awareness and steps to avoid temptation (take your list; eat and drink before you shop so you are not hungry or dehydrated), you may still walk out with things you didn't need or really want. You may back it up with being very convincing in telling yourself that it was worth it, yet that "bargain" may still be sitting on your shelf months or years later.

We Are Conditioned by Our Genes

Even prior to being conceived, you are conditioned by others and your environment. Survival traits are passed on in your DNA in the form of patterns, beliefs, heightened senses, gifts, and talents. Some are useful in providing good instinct or intuitive sense of what is, or is not, good or safe for you... and some are not so useful or relevant today.

Ancestral stressors and traumas are also passed on in your DNA, not just from your parents and grandparents but six or more generations prior. It is actually an ingenious survival adaptation, which means we do not have to experience or test out something to find out if it will kill us, as we innately know. Issues arise when you find yourself reacting irrationally to events, stressors, and things that you do not have a personal experience with or reason for being so scared, fearful, or averse to.

An example of this more recently was seen in the panic buying of toilet paper, where people were fighting for it as if their lives depended on it. Although not necessarily a life-dependant item, it *is* one linked with comfort and may be a hangover from our parents or grandparents when toilet paper and other items were rationed during the war. This is where and how conditioning can become less functional and less appropriate to current environment and conditions.

We can also become entangled and conditioned in our family's stories and history (their conditioning field). Bert Hellinger's *Family Constellations* is an incredible body of work that uncovers and disentangles family conditioning fields created by missing or displaced pieces in the family system.

Family secrets, incomplete pieces, or unfinished business may be carried or taken up by subsequent generations as a means of healing and realigning the family system (tree). You will know if you are the family member who agreed to come and do this work, as you may be interested or obsessed by a past family member's life, feel you need to complete something (such as tell their story), discover you are "living their life," not your own, or your own healing journey will lead you there. Some may feel they have to do something (e.g., join the military or learn to fly) yet it feels misaligned with what they truly want to do. You might discover a great uncle was a pilot or soldier and was killed or missing in action during a war. He may not have been properly grieved or released through a funeral like process by the family (thus creating a vortex you have been drawn into and can heal and realign through ancestral healing).

In constellation work, what might occur is that in the constellation session the great uncle will be acknowledged and honoured within his rightful place in the family system, and once the missing place is filled, you will be free to live your own life with-out being drawn into the family drama or vortex.

It may be useful to have a family constellation if you are a member of a family tree that may have a lot of entanglements due to:

- family secrets, shame, or tragedies that were not talked about or grieved, such as stillbirths, deaths in infancy, abortions, or adoptions.
- family members who are missing or died in war, genocide, tragedy, or disaster, and that feels unresolved or still carries a lot of emotion.
- mental illness or family members committed to mental institutions or imprisoned.
- family members who were disinherited, cast out, or dis-owned by the family.
- misalignment in natural order and roles, like a family member fulfilling a role inappropriate to age, such as children looking after parents or siblings, whether due to hardship, parental absence, death, or inability to parent as a result of dis-ability, illness, or addiction.
- unfinished business and family "wars."

These may present in subsequent generations either as impacting experiences, or as family or genetic diseases, illnesses, or conditions.

Conditioned by Childhood

Before age seven, we exist in an open state of mind, accepting or downloading everything without question. We simply take it in as being true. We may also allocate additional meaning which adds to the programming based on our experience at the time. One of the more common associated meanings added is "I am not good enough," which may become the default until consciously changed. We, however, don't have the power to change for as long as we feel victim to our conditioning.

You may be thinking, *What hope do I have? I am just clogged up with my ancestors' stuff.* However, the sciences of epigenetics and neuroplasticity, plus the increasing research in trauma, show that we are not victims of our genes, mind, or stressors. We have the power to align. We are designed to be self-empowered and joyous. We are evolving to thrive, not just survive.

Conditioning Is Not All "Bad"

Therapeutic circles can give a skewed negative perspective of conditioning—that it is "bad" and we have to change or get rid of it. I would like to offer another perspective.

Conditioning lays down neural pathways or highways that fire more quickly, aiding us in doing things more efficiently or automatically. Conditioning is also why we do not have to learn how to walk or drive a car every time we want to.

We are not *victims* of our conditioning, or at least we do not have to be. There are many miraculous, wonderful, and vital aspects gained from conditioning, like enhanced survival, so let's not get too caught up in negativity here.

It is true that the less aligned we are, or the further we *stray* from our genetic blueprint, the more likely we are to experience the negative feedback of conditioning. This may be through our own or others' negative emotions or behaviours.

So-called negative feedback shows up first as emotions, such as frustration, anger, bitterness, or disappointment, which may escalate to stress, anxiety, or depression and further down the line, as ill-health or disease. The empowering aspect is to consider this feedback as a signpost or invitation, lovingly showing where you are misaligned with your vitality, desires, purpose, dreams, joy, and most wonderful aspects of you.

No, you are not broken. No, you do not need fixing.

You may not even need healing. You are already whole, you already have everything you need, you can realign by being real about what is going on for you by noticing your reactions and responding, rather than just reacting. When you can acknowledge and accept, you are more able to stop yourself from letting the program run you. By changing how you respond this time, your responses may become your new reaction and conditioning next time.

By realigning with your blueprint, you get to be truly *you*. This is the you with all your masks off, who has gifts and talents that come easily. You get to create love, joy, and flow in your life; you get to take your place and be the piece creating your peace.

In order to have a better understanding of who we are and who we are not, we need to understand conditioning: what it is, how it happens, and how it masks our true self.

Before we go further, first here are two foundational concepts that underpin what we are about to explore:

- Everything is energy.
- We experience life through relationships.

Conditioned Energy

If and when we can depersonalise conditioning and simply see it as *energy* and our *relationship* to this energy, it is easier to work with and work through conditioning.

Conditioning causes us to create stories and further entanglements. The ways in which we become entangled with conditioning are when:

- events, happenings, details, or what people say or do are taken personally;

- we get stuck in the story of "what it means;"
- it includes blame, shame, guilt, or traumas;
- it holds deep emotional impact in what happened;
- we give an event or relationship more energy, such as by retelling and reliving it over and over.

By investing more energy in these, we reinforce or create additional conditioning through non-loving behaviours. We need to come to the point we are able to forgive or release the story and entanglements to realign with our true, loving nature.

Keeping emotionally or mentally entangled conditioning in place takes a lot of energy, and sometimes it takes us to the point of exhaustion before we take the steps to release it.

Everything at its true source is energy, and thus we relate to everything energetically. Regardless of what we knock into, experience, perceive, or call it (a person, a thing, an event, a situation), it is energy. Regardless of how we view it, it is energy. And the meaning this energy has for you, is the meaning that *you* give it.

Knowledge is power and this knowledge is powerful, as it can shortcut the process. If you want to change your conditioning, sustain your energy, and focus on what you want (not what you don't want), start by accepting what needs to be changed and stop putting energy into the bad story or giving it more meaning than it has.

Please do not mistake this as suggesting you shouldn't acknowledge the pain of your life stories. Stories are also part of who you are, and they need to be felt to transform the energy; however, they do not have to be relived or dwelt on.

The ultimate question is *what story do you want to tell that helps you align with joy?* (There is an exercise for this later.)

Science of Conditioning

Conditioning includes both sides of the nature/nurture debate:

- genetics
- environment
- energetic openness or empathy
- upbringing and authorities in our lives (parents, family, peers, teachers, law, etc.)
- education, religion, or spiritual practice
- microorganisms in the gut (yes, really, gut bacteria can also influence our choices, especially regarding food!)

When we get down to the energetic level, it is difficult to separate nature from nurture. Let's consider DNA, our energetic code. Traditionally, DNA was considered 100 percent nature. As in, we are born with it, so it is inherited (nature), and it cannot be changed. This has been taken to mean that having certain genes means you will get or be susceptible to certain diseases or traits.

More recently, scientists have discovered lifestyle choices (nurture) can switch genes on or off. Just because you have the gene, does not mean that you will get the disease or trait. The gene may not be switched on, or it may be on, but it might not be activated. Things that can switch on or activate a gene are factors such as stress, diet, and things in our environment such as chemicals and electromagnetic and radiation exposure.

Epigenetics demonstrates that nurture (lifestyle) trumps nature (genetics). This means that how you live and how you behave can turn your genes on or off, activate or deactivate. We can create well-being through lifestyle choices, the more impactful being stress reduction, healthy natural diet (minimal sugar), adequate exercise, sleep, sunlight, and reducing exposure to harmful chemicals and radiation.

Historically, religion has been the main conditioning agent, which has been overtaken by science, medicine, and media today. We used to seek answers from religious texts and leaders, and now we seek answers from science, technology, and media.

To sort the information from misinformation and truth from mis-truth, you need to seek answers from within yourself and be aligned with your own intuition, inner guidance, and truth to have the final say on what is true for you. Science, religion, and media (or more truthfully, we all do this) cherry-pick information for what they want you to know, and what supports your perspective or point of view, thereby extracting the bits that help get the message across or get others to buy what they are selling. In science, scientific "facts" are more about "following the money." Who is paying for the research? What do they want you to know? What do they not really want you to know (fine print), and what are they hiding?

Conditioning and Questions Regarding Health

The area of science that impacts us most today is the medical field. The medical and pharmaceutical viewpoint has conditioned us to consider a medical problem, issue, or symptom as something wrong with us that needs fixing and that only they have the answer. Yet do they? Do we need to question things more?

- Does getting rid of the symptoms mean we are getting rid of the very thing that is showing or guiding us to what, where, or how we can heal and realign with health?
- By getting rid of a symptom, are we hindering, interfering, or stopping the healing process?
- Is cutting something out a cure or just a temporary measure?
- Is our fear of getting a disease, and the preventative measures we take, creating more issues than the disease itself?
- Is our fear of being sick creating the very disease we are trying to avoid?

- Are the potential dangers, risks, and side effects of treatment or medication actually worse than the diagnosed issue?
- Is prevention truly better than cure?
- What is prevention and what is intervention?
- Is anything safe and effective for everyone?
- Do we need to see doctors as people, rather than gods in white coats who can make our life-or-death decisions?
- With so much money going to cancer research, why is cancer *more* common, not less?
- Are we being deceived into believing there is a magical cure or pill that can fix us without having to do anything but swallow it?
- Is conditioning, information overload, busyness, apathy, laziness, overwhelm, or trauma playing into our health and lifestyle choices today?
- When you make decisions regarding your health, what voices play out in your head to arrive at that decision?

I ask these questions, as I believe there are many answers. Questions like these are important to ask so we do not take in conditioning blindly. In some cases, our conditioning will work *for* us, in some, it will not. What is right and works for one, is not right and may not work for another; make choices that feel aligned for you.

Conditioning and Evolution

For a balanced view of conditioning, let's look at it from an evolutionary point of view. From the genetic aspect, human conditioning has been a vital feature of survival. Genetics is more than just what we look like or the conditions we may inherit from our parents and ancestors. Through our DNA, we have the potential to inherit the traumas and unresolved issues of our ancestors. We also have the *potential* to inherit the gifts, talents, lessons, and adaptations, the very survival skills and wisdom that enabled them to pass on their DNA to their children.

Ancestral wisdom is passed through genes, so we do not have to experience or test it out for ourselves. It may show up as aversions or heightened sensitivity to certain tastes or smells, fear, phobias, or anxiety around things, which have no reference to our own lives, or something that may have made our ancestor unwell or killed someone close to them. The wisdom of nature means we may not have to suffer the same fate. The objective at the non-personal energetic level of parenting is for future generations to have a better life and to give the next generation the best start by not having to start from scratch.

We inherit heightened intuitive senses, skills, gifts, and talents that can be used in many ways and may become an integral expression of who we are. A heightened sense of hearing may deliver a gifted ear for music. A profound sense of smell may be why you are an amazing chef, or you have the ability to "smell a rat" and have such great business acumen.

We also become conditioned by family patterns. We adopt programmed patterns, fears, and beliefs of caregivers, teachers, peers, government, industry, religion, organisations, media, or anything or anyone we view as an authority. When a pattern is healthy, it offers a sense of stability or assurance. When a pattern is not so healthy, we can opt out, which, yes, can be simple in theory and less easy in practice, especially when we're unaware of the pattern, or it is culturally or socially accepted and reinforced.

We cannot escape conditioning, as we are constantly in relationship with our environment and others and thus constantly subject to the various types of conditioning. In any relationship we have with anyone or anything, we exchange energy, which creates the conditions of that relationship.

It helps to become confident in trusting ourselves in finding our own way to be in the world and how we interact with it. It is becoming increasingly known that things are not quite how they seem or how we have been told. We need to become rebels and stop trying to be "normal" or fit in with "social norms" as really there is no such thing.

Let go of the concept of *normal*. You do not know what influence or impact you have. You do not know how you can shake up or inspire someone, somewhere, or somehow simply by being yourself.

Not one of us naturally fits into the conditioned constructs of society, as it is a construct! You need to stop believing that you should, or that you even can, "fit in." If this is not full permission to stop making yourself wrong about not fitting into a box (that nobody can fit into) I do not know what is. Stop searching for something you ARE already!

Realigning Exercise: Why Do You Do It?

It is not our specific behaviours or actions that indicate conditioning, it is *why* we do it.

- Are you doing it because of social, cultural, or other pressures? Or, are you doing it because it is aligned with your personal freedom, experience, or expression?
- Is your behaviour or actions an expression of you or of social requirements?
- Is it aligned with spirit or social order?
- Do you do it because of social conditioning or for self-actualisation?

- Are your actions dictated in order *to be accepted* for who or how you are?
  Or, are your actions directed because *of acceptance* of who or how you are?

A key indicator is feeling how it feels.

- Does it feel conditioned or natural?
- Does it feel restrictive and contractive (conditioned) or expansive and evolving (natural)?
- Does it feel habitual, automatic, reactive, static (conditioned), or flowing, innovative, responsive, or fluid (natural)?

For example:

- Do you keep your house clean because you are worried what others may think and to present a certain standing or because a clean house feels good and gives you a sense of order or satisfaction?
- Are you reading that book to appear knowledgeable or well versed, or are you reading it because you are curious and want to know more?
- Are you working at a job because it provides status or money, or because it provides you freedom to do what you want?
- Are you watching that foreign film to be more cultured, or because it is personally fascinating?
- Are you going to the party because you think you should, or because you want to?
- Are you wearing that dress/suit because it will attract the attention of others or because it feels good and expresses who you are?
- Are you being of support to another for how it will look, or for how it will feel?

Natural or unconditioned actions do not always feel good and easy. In fact, they more often feel scary because freedom is our greatest fear. What you are looking for is that it feels aligned with you and your sense of personal freedom. Deconditioning is the freedom to consciously choose your actions and behaviours.

Realigning Exercise:
Who Is Telling My Story?

Grab your journal or voice recorder and allocate fifteen to thirty minutes of uninterrupted time for contemplation. If it helps to set an alarm so you can fully focus, please do so.

Think of a story you have told more than a few times, or a story that you find yourself telling often that you would like to reframe. Write it down or dictate your story with a voice recorder.

Now review what you have written or recorded and notice when you tell this story or share about yourself and your experiences:

- Are you able to notice who or which part (persona or archetype) is telling the story?
- Does it feel like a wounded, hurt, or healthy aspect of yourself?
- Does it feel like it's coming from a younger you? How old?
- If you were an actor, archetype, or cartoon figure, who would you be?
- Why, or for what purpose, are you telling this story in this way?
- What do you hope to gain or have acknowledged by telling it?

For example:

If you find you are regularly telling a story about your medical conditions, illness, diseases, injuries, or wounding, is the story coming from the perspective of the victim or wounded child? Or is it coming from the healed or healing aspect of self, such as from a healer or teacher perspective?

- Which part is telling the story and is it because it is seeking empathy or emotional energy of others?

- Which part is seeking this energy and is it because it does not feel it can source it for itself?

- Which part is attempting to create intimacy by sharing wounding (rather than vulnerability)?

- Is the story being told by a part wanting to be confident? Is it a part that builds a story so others can see how good it is when deep down it needs to feel convinced it is good enough?

- Is the story coming from an empowered part that appreciates the challenges and experiences it has faced and how it has navigated them? Is it an honest appreciation of what it took to get through? Or is it a story that may (unintentionally or intentionally) inspire, guide, or assist others?

- Or is the story coming from a part that simply wants to share a story or experience? And does the real joy come from the experience of sharing wisdom that may assist another?

- If it is coming from a disempowered or wounded aspect of self, can you imagine a different possibility or a more empowering story?

- How would you like to change your story?

- What part could tell your story in a more empowered, humble, or aligned way?

Realigning Exercise:
Reframing Your Story

This exercise can be done as the second part of the previous exercise, or it can be done by itself.

A powerful way to reframe or reinvent your story of adversity is to tell it in a way that is more inspiring or powerful. You may use complete fantasy, analogy, or fiction, telling your story in a different way.

An example:

A story I told in a workshop was how I was all over the place and had so many things on the go that I was unable to focus on one thing or get anything done as well or perfectly as I wanted to and how that was making me feel depressed and unhappy with myself.

The story that was retold to me by my partner has stuck in my mind ever since. She reframed my "all over the place" story into something like this:

There was a gardener who had a garden with many garden beds, each filled with flowers and some weeds. She tended to each garden bed when she could, doing a little bit here and a little bit there.

She was looking at one garden bed and wished she could do more and tend to it and make it perfect. As she looked in despair at the garden bed with a few flowers and all those weeds, she noticed the bees, birds, and beetles tending to different plants.

She widened her gaze and saw all the beautiful flowers blooming in all the garden beds. The weeds were no longer weeds; they were important elements, adding life, vigour, and colour to the garden.

She had created a garden and ecosystem, not just a garden bed. She was able to walk through an entire garden, not just sit by a single garden bed. She had given life to and tended to many things, not just one. There was beauty beyond a garden bed, there was beauty everywhere.

How could you rewrite your story?

Attachment and Authenticity

Something that may be useful in understanding why we get conditioned in the ways we do is to understand the intelligence behind it. I feel a lot can be explained by Attachment Theory, first described by psychiatrist John Bowlby.

The essence of this theory is that as infants we engage in instinctive behaviours that create attachment, to avoid separation from caregivers whom we are totally reliant on for our survival.

How this relates to conditioning is that there are two basic choices we make, attachment (relationships to others) or authenticity (relationship to self). As infants, choices that ensure attachment to caregivers are prioritised in order to survive. In many cases, attachment may be in lieu of or in detriment to authentic choices less immediate to survival. As children, we make ourselves wrong, as it is less threatening than to believe our caregivers are.

As we get older and rely less on others for our every need, choices to create attachment may become dysfunctional or even harmful to us. This includes behaviours such as people pleasing, codependency, putting others' needs before our own, not questioning others' motives, weak boundaries, negative self-image, and self-critical behaviours, any of which may leave us feeling lost, disconnected, misunderstood, anxious, or resentful.

As we go through various life stages, our need and call to be more ourselves will emerge, especially at midlife crisis points around the ages of thirty, forty, and fifty. This is when our conditioning can feel particularly gnarly.

Remember that all the conditioning and behaviours you are now having difficulty with, at one stage performed a very vital and important role, as they ensured your survival. Thank yourself for being so intelligent. Now use this same intelligence to notice and change your conditioning to find healthier ways of attachment and relationship, while also realigning with what is authentic to you and considers your needs. You no longer need to just survive; you can thrive by being you.

Realigning Exercise:
Attachment or Authenticity?

Review from a big picture or thematic way. Feel (rather than think) whether your primary objective or behaviour was to achieve attachment or achieve authenticity at the various ages listed below. Circle or highlight for each age to your current age.

0-2	Attachment	Authenticity
2-6	Attachment	Authenticity
6-12	Attachment	Authenticity
12-16	Attachment	Authenticity
16-18	Attachment	Authenticity
18-21	Attachment	Authenticity
22-29	Attachment	Authenticity
30-40	Attachment	Authenticity
40-50	Attachment	Authenticity

| 50-60 | Attachment | Authenticity |
| 60+ | Attachment | Authenticity |

What do you notice?

What would you say is your primary driver?

Have you been able to achieve attachment *and* authenticity in some or most areas in your life?

——————————— 〜〜—————————

With loving curiosity, can you recollect any behaviours or choices in the last year that were for the primary objective to create attachment with another?

Examples of less functional attachment behaviours might include:

- people pleasing
- martyrdom
- going out of your way and inconveniencing yourself
- saying "it doesn't matter" when it really does
- pretending you were not hurt by another's actions or words
- caring for another at great expense to your own well-being
- proving yourself to others
- being a servant (rather than being *of* service)
- acting how you think others want you to act
- being who, or how, others want you to be

Pick one of the behaviours and take a few minutes to simply be with how you feel about it without changing, criticising, or fixing.

Did it feel like you were compromising your authenticity and self-esteem?

Can you accept that this behaviour had intelligence behind it at some time in your life, such as keeping you safe?

If you would like to, what would change?

In what ways could you act more authentically next time?

What possibilities can you imagine might help achieve both relationship *and* authenticity?

How We Are Conditioned by Others

It is important to understand the effect another's presence has on your energy and sense of self. It is not something to fear or loathe, as there are many ways we can also utilise it because learning is conditioning. Awareness in conditioning can be worked with, especially in terms of getting to know yourself and understand what is true for you, as we get to know ourselves through relationships.

Our bodies have an energetic field (called an aura) that extends about a metre around us. When our auric field meets the auric field of another, energy is exchanged and mixed. In this way, our auric field becomes conditioned by the other and vice versa.

Often referred to as *empathy*, another's aura can condition and influence or impact your decisions, emotions, and choices and you may find you think or feel quite differently about something when no longer in the aura of another.

We cannot and do not want to avoid others or conditioning. However, it is also beneficial to remove yourself from the conditioning field of others' auras when making important decisions, so you can align with what is correct and joyous for you.

We are all empathic to varying degrees; it is through this nature we pick up emotions, thoughts, or energy of those around us. This in itself is not a problem as empathy is how we take others in and is a vital part of relating with and understanding others. It's only a problem when we identify or confuse other people's emotions, thoughts, or energy as our own. For some, this can be confusing, as we may feel the other more strongly and acutely than the self.

Knowing how the energy of others influences your own can be used to advantage. You may find that thoughts flow more easily and creatively when you are in public spaces and thus have access to other people's ideas and energy making it easier for you to connect thoughts.

If someone's or something's energy does not feel good, it can be advantageous to break energy completely or for fifteen minutes to decondition and realign with your own centre. It can make a huge difference in the outcome of a situation. Although you may feel the pressure to sort out whatever is in front of you at the time, or you might be conscious of offending them, do not be afraid or ashamed to ask for space so you can realign with how you feel.

Paradoxically, we are all one, so our conditioning is as much about who we are as it is about who we are not. We learn who we are and what our values and truths are through contrast and relationship.

Unfortunately, much of our cultural conditioning and its love for labels, boxes, and categories leads us away from ourselves and our source of joy as we try to fit them. A lot of conditioning intends to make us more manageable or homogenous, more like others than like our individual unique and empowered selves.

Joy arises through connecting with and expressing the truth of who we are. Our conditioning is also part of who we are. We cannot escape it, nor should we want to, yet we do need to be aware of and work with it, as conditioning energy is powerful in many ways and can transfix or transform us. Create conditioning that promotes love and joy for you and others.

Program yourself with the conditions and conditioning of your choosing (how you want to be and feel).

Realigning Exercise:
What Is Your Conditioning?

We are more likely to be conditioned through or via certain mediums.

With certain people, groups, phases, or places, are you aware whether you:

- think or behave differently?
- have access to certain abilities you do not usually?
- do or say things you would not normally?
- feel a change of mood or wonder why you feel so different?
- feel more certain or excited about a project—and later wonder *What was I thinking?*
- find your thoughts are clearer?
- express yourself more, or less, easily?
- like working or feel more creative or inspired in public spaces, such as libraries or cafes?
- eat more, or emotionally eat?

Awareness of how you are conditioned by others and how you condition others, can help you work with the naturally occurring energetic exchanges more consciously and powerfully. There may be ways we can use this field to strengthen our gifts or utilise this group energy consciously with greater advantage to all.

Relationships are, at their core, energetic exchanges and negotiations of power, so questions to ask could be:

- Do I feel overpowered? Am I overpowering others? = (power *over*)
- Do I feel mutual energetic exchange? = (power *with*)
- Do we each feel energised? = (amplified mutual exchange)
- Do I feel balanced and like myself? = (balanced or neutral)

- Do I (or they) feel wired or tired? = (amplified unmanaged energies)
- Do I (or they) feel drained? = (energy leaks or grabs)

Remember true power in relationships is mutual exchange—power with, not power over—when coming together makes each feel better and happier within themselves.

Knowing how your energy is transmitted and received is vital to understanding your relationships. If you find certain people or groups leave you feeling drained, overwhelmed, hijacked, or manipulated, it may be beneficial to work out ways you can better protect yourself and your energy.

If the exchange feels a bit one-sided (i.e., all take rather than give), you may want to consider engaging more consciously. This might include limiting the time you spend with them, whether that is in duration, or only at times you have the energy and presence to remain yourself. Discovering your tipping point (where healthy exchange becomes unhealthy) is vital in relationships and may be managed simply by quietly excusing yourself for a short time to regain your composure or removing yourself entirely when you feel the shift or tipping point.

Remember that relationships are long-term investments and part of balance is see-sawing both ways to come back to centre. Some-times exchange may be one-sided, such as times of crisis when offering support. The questions may be as follows:

- Does it balance out over time?
- Are you or are they constantly seeking or expecting support or help?

Or maybe the bigger questions:

- Do you allow yourself to be supported by them?
- Do you ask for their help when you need it?

- Is it you who is creating or fostering a one-sided relationship?
- Are they pulling away, or are you?

Realigning with Joy

There are many roads we can take towards change, growth, and self-improvement.

We have been conditioned to take the highway of pain and suffering, only detouring off the road when the pain or effort of changing feels less than the pain or effort of continuing on the road we were on.

What if we were to introduce another road—the path of joy—where motivation is not sourced from pain or suffering? Instead, the joyous path comes from the inspiration to breathe in the enjoyment of life, from the momentum of feeling good, and from the willingness and exquisite boldness to express your creative gifts and talents. It is the path that has the vision of creative adventure, the ambition and determination to be healthy, the hunger for freedom, the willingness and determination to *be* who you truly are—a much-loved, joyous, precious, and beautiful being.

It is time to create consciously and move towards what *you are* (which IS love and joy), rather than running away or trying to escape what you do not want or who you do not really want to be (which is the path of pain).

It hurts to sit on the fence too long; at some stage we need to make a move to one side or the other to get off it. Do not worry if what you first create is not quite what you want. You get to tweak and recreate as you learn and grow. Do not let the fear stop you.

Yes, it feels very real… yet, it is not. You do *not* need to know everything, be certain, or be perfect. Just hop down off the fence.

The road of healing in the medical sense is commonly associated with effort, pain, struggle, suffering, and sourcing things external to you. However, the path of realigning can be joyful, effortless, and fun. It involves a more internal process of accessing the template you were born with, your blueprint, your own personal architecturally designed home that is your body in all dimensions.

Realigning (or "REALigning") means getting real, seeing past the delusions and lies we have been fed in order to be controllable, or more like them (and less like ourselves). Stop believing the lies that you are not good enough in some way or that you must behave in a certain way to be loved, or that you are not precious, special, powerful, and unlimited. These are lies we have *all* been fed even before our conception.

It's about REALigning with the truth that:

- *you are love*; you are loved, loving, and lovable, and that your true Source and the source of your power is pure unconditional love;
- The Universe cares for you, and conspires *with* you and *for* you, not *against* you;
- you are more powerful and divinely gifted than you realise; and;
- you are never alone and have never been separate from your divine source as you are a part of *the* Divine Source.

You are loved unconditionally. You are worthy, deserving, and valuable simply for being you. You do not have to do anything to be loved, worthy, or deserving. **You already are!**

Realigning Exercise:
Conditioning

Pick a field of conditioning:

- parenting
- authority
- school, education
- news, media, advertising
- social media
- religion
- social, culture
- family, ancestral
- genetic

Contemplate and/or experiment with:

- How has it conditioned, impacted, or affected you negatively?
- How has it conditioned, impacted, or affected you positively?
- How can you work with it in a way that assists or empowers you?
- Is there something you need to accept about it?
- We are all conditioned, including the people or things that condition us. With this understanding, is there anything or anyone to forgive?
- What do you need to forgive yourself for?

When You Get Hijacked

The most influential conditioning comes from media, including the news, social media, and advertising. The objective is to create an emotional response, especially the lower frequency emotions such as fear, shame, and guilt. Media and advertising rely heavily on fear, guilt, shame, insecurity, inadequacy, comparison, and feeling not good enough. Why? Because in these states we are more easily manipulated as we are more in the survival reflexes, which means less blood gets to the brain, thus making us more vulnerable to being coerced into believing or buying something as we are not thinking coherently.

We are in our heads, but not in a conscious way, and we are in our lower emotional energy making it easier to sway or convince us to buy a product, system, or solution, so we can *temporarily* feel better about ourselves, fit in, be good, feel happy, strong, or successful, and not miss out. You name it! There are all manner of ways to manipulate behaviour.

Few people make effective decisions, choices, or purchases under pressure. The sales tactic of "buy now or miss out" can quickly hijack our senses, and we find ourselves buying stuff we don't truly need or even want. We may feel excited and smart for getting a bargain, but it's a bargain that may later cost us in buyers' remorse that outlives and outweighs the short thrill.

Advertising and media have all the tricks, bells, and whistles to manipulate your energy. They know what they are doing, and they do it extremely well. There is a whole science and psychological formula behind it.

How do you avoid the trap? *WAIT!* Yes, just wait. Pause and do not buy on impulse—unless you are one of the rare few who can and do buy well on impulse. Have an honest review of your purchase history to see if you are an effective instinctual buyer.

You can know all the traps and know where they are and still get caught. On many occasions I have been hijacked by energetic sales assistants on days when I felt under pressure, anxious, emotionally sensitive, hungry, or dehydrated.

I have paid full colour printing for black and white (without saying anything), bought something even though I knew they were spinning me lies (and not called them on it because I did not want to be rude), bought stuff because I didn't want to miss out (and never used it), and bought a couch in the colour someone else liked (even though they did not live with me).

If I had simply taken a time-out, walked away, stopped to acknowledge my discomfort, spoken up, or asked for time to reconsider *before* buying, I may have made different choices and decisions. If I had enough self-presence to not get swept up by friendly, bubbly sales assistants who were good at their job, I may have saved a lot of money or asked for what I actually wanted. If I had eaten before going food shopping, I may not have filled up my basket with junk and likely made different—better—choices... and I also would not be sharing these stories with you now.

When I have a clear vision or plan of what I want and allow myself the space and time needed, I make better choices. When I ensure I am fed, hydrated, and on an even keel, unafraid to miss out, say no or stop, or say "I will get back to you" or "let me sleep on it," I have made purchases and choices I was happy with at the time *and* long after. I have even bought things that may stir up joy when I connect with them.

Realigning Exercise: When Do *You* Get Hijacked?

———————◦◦◦———————

There are a few times that I have bought something and when I got it home have gone, "What the _____? Why did I buy this?"

Have you been caught out and bought something you did not want, or agreed to something you did not resonate with, just because you:

- feared you might miss out (FOMO);
- feared what they might think of you or say about you;
- did not want to say no, or could not say no;
- did not want to say no again—after your *no* was ignored, invalidated, rejected, ridiculed, or made fun of;
- did not want to ask questions in case you appeared stupid, silly, or foolish;
- felt under the spell of the sale or salesperson (glamoured, coerced, bullied);
- got talked into or talked around (convinced when you were not internally convinced);
- did not want to upset or put someone out;
- felt guilty, ashamed, or "less than" in some way;
- felt vulnerable or emotionally sensitive;
- felt excited or caught up in the hype (everybody else is raving about it);
- were in a hurry or feeling like you are running out of time;
- felt under pressure or pressured (you'd do anything to make the pressure go away);

- wanted to escape, get out, get it over and done with;
- felt exhausted, fatigued, tired, or over stretched;
- were starving, hungry, or hangry (angry hungry);
- were thirsty or dehydrated;
- felt distracted in or by other thoughts, concerns, or happenings;
- felt confused, doubtful, bamboozled, or didn't want to look stupid;
- wanted connection of some kind or wanted to be part of "it;"
- wanted to fit in or create attachment to another in some way;
- wanted to impress, get in with the in-crowd, or be part of the craze; or
- thought you were being smart, getting a great bargain, and saving money (even though you didn't need or want it, or even know how to use it or what it was for)?

Do I need to go on…?

Maintaining a sense of humour and kindness towards yourself, while being aware of the situations or circumstances under which you are more vulnerable or open to manipulation, or having your good and common senses overruled or hijacked may help you navigate these types of situations more skilfully next time.

If you are able to enter into the situation, purchase, contract, or relationship with cleaner energy, you are less likely to be side-swiped by it, or you might catch yourself before it is too late.

And remember,

- No matter how well prepared, you can still get caught out.
- Be kind and gentle with yourself.
- Although you may think punishing yourself means you will not do or will be less likely to do it again, it actually makes it more likely as it is in your field (and remember, the nervous system likes what it's already survived).

- Forgiveness creates enduring change (much better than punishment).
- A good sense of humour helps.
- Get comfortable saying no to what you want or need to say no to and yes to what you need or want to say yes to.

Possibly *the* thing that may help the most is practicing and becoming comfortable saying:

"Let me sleep on it, before I make that decision."

Do not be afraid to give yourself extra time to make important decisions. Very few people make excellent decisions spontaneously or under pressure, especially on the big things.

Realigning Exercise:
Emotional Manipulation

A good emotion-evoking story is an effective tool for teaching and creating change as emotional engagement makes it more memorable. It can also persuade or manipulate towards a desired outcome or mental conclusion. It can be so obvious and also so subversive we may be unaware of it.

Let's look at how our emotions can be directed (or manipulated) by story.

Show 1 is following a herd of gazelles.

We have been told their story of survival and how they function as a herd. We feel like we know them. We have watched them escape danger and near death. We have watched them have babies. Some have not made it. They are grazing after an exhausting day crossing flooded rivers where some did not make it. They are hungry. The camera pans out to a lioness watching and waiting in the long grass. An exhausted gazelle and her baby fawn walk dangerously near...

What do you think happens next?

What emotions and thoughts are arising?

How would you feel about a different or opposite outcome?

Any different emotions or thoughts arising?

Who do you feel the most connected with or concerned for? The gazelle, lion, or fawn?

Would it make any difference if it was a lone gazelle, or if she did not have a baby?

Show 2 is following a lone lioness.

We have been told her story of survival and how she has been cast out of the pride. We feel like we know her. We have watched her escape danger and near death. We have watched her have six cubs; most did not make it. She is quietly watching and waiting after two days of failed hunts. She and her two cubs are hungry. The camera pans out to a herd of gazelles grazing the long grass. An exhausted gazelle and her fawn walk temptingly near...

What do you think happens next?

What emotions and thoughts are arising?

How would you feel about the opposite outcome?

Any different emotions or thoughts arising?

Who do you feel the most connected with or concerned for? The gazelle, lion, or cub?

Would it make any difference if she was with a pride of lions, not a lone lioness, or without cubs?

What Are You Buying Into?

Today, we are drowning in information, yet lacking in wisdom. You access *your* wisdom (and your joy) when you connect with what is true and correct for you, not by following the narrative.

We have been educated, conditioned, spellbound, and brainwashed by news, advertising, and media—all with their own agenda: to buy their product or buy into their point of view. And yes, this book is no different!

It is important to learn to connect with what *feels* right and true for you and follow that. It's also important to read the emotional energy that is stirred from reading between the lines, rather than just the line being fed. Agendas can be obvious or transparent (and thus also easily missed), and they can be masterfully hidden or manipulative. This is why you need to *feel* into how aligned you are with what you are reading, watching, and taking in.

Whether others are individuals, corporations, the collective, religions, or institutions, find the joy in making decisions correct for *you*, rather than buying into *their* agendas.

When I say "buying into," I am speaking of believing something you may not otherwise believe, or "selling yourself out" by compromising your ideals, beliefs, or values in some way. You can feel it when you do—it might feel a bit icky or may trigger guilt, regret, unworthiness, or other states or emotions that do not sit well or feel right. Buyer's remorse is due to misalignment. It can be a good purchase or choice; however, if there is remorse, there are emotions or feelings that have not been attended to or aligned.

A key to "not getting bought" or not buying into something you do not actually believe in, is to question everything and stay curious. It is easy to lose connection or feel we do not know what our inner truth is, as the tactics used in advertising, informing, or selling often invoke feelings of guilt, shame, fear, and inadequacy (emotions that make us feel *less*; i.e., less likely to trust ourselves and more likely to buy into or go along with their narrative).

When we make another person, organisation, or thing an authority in our lives, we lose connection with the joy of our own authority. There is a huge difference between following or obeying some-one blindly or under duress and following someone with conscious choice aligned with your truth.

When you let someone or something have authority over you, it erodes self-esteem, self-confidence, and joy. For example, have you ever judged yourself or your actions harshly, been too hard on yourself, or thought you would become a better person if you were tougher with yourself? Yet have you ever considered that *being critical, harsh, or hard on yourself actually makes you more critical, harsh, and hard... not better or kinder!*

Few escape the feeling of "not good enough" in some way (not smart enough, pretty enough, thin enough, or fat enough). The "not enough" we may truly be guilty of, is not enjoying being ourselves enough.

Consider buying into the fact that you are adult enough to have the power to choose your truth. We live in an exciting and privileged time where we have access to spiritual wisdom once only accessible to those in the highest orders of religion. Today, we do not have to choose between the spiritual or the mundane path. We can be spiritual *and* be in the real (mundane) world. We can be corporate hippies, industrial gurus, and podcasting priests and priestesses.

We are living in a time where we can realign with the higher truth of who we are: a divine spiritual being having a physical experience, a cocreator with Christ consciousness with the capacity to create miracles and share the truth of who we are.

Buy into being someone who knows the difference between following another's lead because it feels aligned with you, versus thinking they know more or better than you. Recognise when you comply for the greater good, versus complying to *be* good.

Be aware of what you are buying into and when you buy from *not enough*.

We do not need *more* lack or fear in the world (which drives competition and consumerism). The world needs love and joy. We are actually designed to have all we need in life; are you willing to ask and receive it?

Realigning Exercise:
A Few Questions to Contemplate

- What things do you feel guilty about?
- What beliefs have you been buying into that activate feelings of guilt?
- When was the last time you felt shame?
- What were you buying into or believing to activate that shame?

If you are having difficulty, think in terms of where you may have felt inadequate or not enough. What beliefs are you buying into or taking on, that are not true for you or do not serve you?

Common "buy ins" might be:

- Must work hard to make a living.
- Deserve money only if worked hard for it.
- It is wrong to cry or be angry.
- Crying is a sign of weakness.
- Feelings are something to feel guilty or ashamed of.
- It is wrong to say no.
- Must be nice to everyone.
- Being honest is being rude.
- It does not matter if I break promises to myself, as long as I keep promises to others.

For anything that you are buying into:

1. Allow yourself to sit with the feeling without changing or forcing anything. Just notice. Where do you feel it in your body when you believe this?

   Feel into whether you need to know where you first heard this. Sometimes it helps to understand, sometimes it does not. Trust whichever one it is.

2. Does this feeling have anything to say? Does it have a message?
   Allow what wants to arise to arise without judgement. It may be recent or from another time, even before birth. Simply allow and trust what you get (whether it makes sense or not).

3. Just sit with it for at least two minutes. Longer if needed, until you feel it "let go of you" or shift, or until you feel more at peace or calm.

4. When you reread the statement you were working on, does it have any pull or activate any emotions anymore?

If no, your work is complete.

If yes, allow more time to simply sit and observe it.

When we allow the time to simply observe, acknowledge, and accept how we are feeling without judging it or trying to change it, it transforms, moves on, or changes all by itself. All that is required of you is loving presence or witnessing.

What Mind Are You In?

We actually have three "minds." The brain in our head is not the only mind we have. There are also two body-minds which are the heart and gut (solar plexus). The brain is not *just* where conscious-ness lives; our entire body has consciousness. (Remember: matter is energy and consciousness.)

The heart and gut actually have more neural pathways for receiving information from our environment than the brain. The heart and gut, as sensing organs, have a better sense and capacity to gather information to determine what is best for us. The brain's function is to analyse the information *and follow directives from* the heart and gut to initiate action and communicate it with others.

The brain in our head is not actually designed to make decisions, yet we have been taught to make decisions using the mind, to make lists and apply logic and reason; however, the mind is not to be trusted in this function, as the mind is fickle and changes.

The brain only knows what it knows or what it has learned. It does not know our future direction or purpose. The brain, although it may know a lot, is not actually wise. Wisdom is embodied know-ledge and learning, so it is more precisely the body that is wise. The mind's role is important; however, its skill is in creating the words so we can communicate and share the body's wisdom.

The human mind has a natural bias towards the negative and preparing for the worst, as it has ensured our survival. The brain-mind can trap us in the lower-quality aspects of fear, such as doubt, suspicion, confusion, and psychosis (which are not really "real" as they are all created by thinking). We do not need to allow our primitive, reptilian, fear-driven, survival brains to run the show. It is time we relocate and become more conscious and intuitive, utilising our wiser guiding minds that are able to connect with our future and sense our environment (our heart and gut).

The brain cannot truly understand the infinite or what cannot be explained. The body-mind or intuitive senses, however, can *know* something to be true without having to understand, explain, or have reason for it. It is the body-mind that connects and aligns choices with joy, not just happiness.

Realigning Exercise:
The Three Chairs

This exercise helps you to get out of your head and into your body. When the mind is too concerned with which is which, or what is what, it makes it hard to make a choice, so we are best to allow our body to "read the room."

It is easier to access the other brains (heart and gut) and tune in with intuition (which knows the unknown) when you know you cannot rely on your mind to know what is what.

And how will you know what the best option is? Just like Goldilocks, you are finding the chair that feels just right.

This exercise may be helpful to:

- Make decisions between specific choices, like houses, holidays, situations, jobs, purchases, relationships, life changes, or anything.
- Clarify how you feel about certain choices.

- Determine what is best, or whether to do something.
- Gain or access guidance or direction on any choice or decision.

You will need:

3 (+) pieces of paper (envelopes optional) and pen

3 (+) chairs (same or different)

 (+) suggest maximum six options and chairs (or it becomes too confusing)

Step Overview:

1. Clarify your question and options and set the three chairs (or "field") by stating your intention or question and asking for highest guidance.
2. Write each option on a separate piece of paper.
3. Write "other" on a piece of paper also (to allow for better options or clarity).
4. Fold each piece of paper, so they are all the same shape and size (or put them in envelopes).
5. Shuffle or mix papers (or envelopes) so you don't know which is which, then randomly place one per chair.
6. Take a few breaths, create a calm, neutral state mentally and emotionally, and refocus your attention on your goal, then see or feel if a particular chair stands out or draws you (or just select a chair at random) and sit on it.
7. How does it feel? Notice any instinctive reactions or thoughts. Notice comfort level, temperature, body sensations, emotions, and energy. Notice how you feel overall and how you sit in or on the chair over the course of the exercise. (Refer to example for more detail.)
   Are you getting any additional information?
   Are there any questions you feel to ask for greater clarity?

8. When you have enough information from this chair (option) you may choose or sit in the next chair for comparison.

9. Repeat steps 7 and 8 until it feels like you have your answer, or all the chairs are done.

10. Without thinking about it, intuitively feel the right choice, then unfold (or open the envelope). Notice how you feel upon reading it, as this is also valuable information.

11. Thank the chairs or field for the guidance and pick up the rest of the papers to close the inquiry. If you need to do another one, have a break first to clear the space and start from step 1 to reset your intentions.

Let's work through an example and provide more detail to the above:

Inquiry: Where is the best place to have a fun and restful holiday?

Options: Tasmania or Thailand?

(You may wish to be more specific in options, such as region, city, resort, hotel, or type of accommodation.)

Step 1: Choose three chairs and set them up in a line or circle.

The chairs can be the same, such as three dining chairs or can be a mix of chairs of different shapes, sizes, and degrees of comfort.

Note: Chairs may feel different from usual (e.g., comfortable may feel uncomfortable, soft may feel hard).

Take a few slow deep breaths. Calm your body and mind to feel as neutral emotionally and mentally as possible. Take a few moments to consider or clarify your inquiry and the options to explore.

Set and open the field by stating your intention and asking for assistance from the highest source to help guide you to the best choice or decision.

Step 2: When you feel happy with the inquiry and options, write on separate pieces of paper:

- Tasmania (Option A)
- Thailand (Option B)
- Other

Step 3: *Other* enables other possibilities (e.g., more suitable destinations) or options, as this technique accommodates for what we do not (or could not) know. *Other* might activate if:

- foreseeing of conditions at the time of the holiday is unsuitable (e.g., storms, strikes, or other situations);
- a more suitable destination (choice) needs to be considered;
- other things might impact the holiday or choice;
- the inquiry or options are not clear; or
- something, such as the intention or options, needs to be tweaked.

As *other* can represent many things, ask, listen to, and trust your gut in regard to what it might be. If you feel you are not getting anything, sleep on it and allow the answer to come to you. Remember: Do not think—allow it to rise into your thoughts.

Step 4: Fold each paper, so all look the same and you cannot see what is written. For additional secrecy, if you think you are going to peek or cheat or if you want to enjoy the reveal, you can place each into its own envelope.

Step 5: Shuffle or mix them up, so you do not know which is which. Place each paper or envelope on its own chair (one chair = one option).

Step 6: Take a few slow, deep breaths to calm the body and mind and help feel more neutral emotionally and mentally. Then stand back, face the chairs, and refocus the question in your mind. If it helps, place one hand over your heart and the other over your belly to help you tune into your body and get out of your head.

Look at all three chairs and see if one chair stands out (looks brighter, more appealing, attractive, or different), or if you feel or sense any chair inviting or pulling you towards it. If so, go to that chair and sit on it. If you are not feeling anything, choose any chair.

Step 7: While sitting on the chair, tune in to how it feels, how you are feeling and how you are feeling sitting in the chair? What are you sensing or feeling? What thoughts or emotions are arising? Do you notice things like:

- Comfort or discomfort:
  - Do you want to jump out of the chair, or sink into it?
  - Does it feel hard, soft, or medium?
  - Does it feel inviting, repelling, or somewhere in between?
  - Do you feel restless, or find it hard to sit still?
  - Does it feel different than expected (such as a soft chair feeling hard or hard feeling soft, a huggy armchair feeling constrictive or vacant, a plain chair feeling luxurious)?

- Temperature:
  - Does the chair feel hot, cold, warm, or different to room temperature?
  - Do you feel hot, cold, warm, or different than before?

- Body sensations:
  - Do you feel pain in places not felt prior to sitting?
  - Do you feel waves of energy?
  - Does your energy feel constricted or expanded?
  - Does it feel good... or not?

- Did you or do you smell, taste, or hear anything unusual?
- Did you or do you have any gut reactions?

- Rising emotions or feelings:
  - Do you feel unusually excited? Or sad or depressed?
  - Do you have more or less energy?
  - Is your energy being revitalised or drained?

- Emerging thoughts, ideas, insights, or images:
  - Is anything coming to your awareness?
  - Do you feel or think that you know which one it is?

- Additional information or data:
  - Are you getting any additional awareness?
  - Do you feel you know which option it is?

- Nothing: you feel, sense, or get nothing.

Overall, do you (and thus this option) feel bad or good? Does it feel unfavourable or favourable, wrong or right? How you and/or the chair feels is an indication of how the holiday will feel at that destination. If you do not feel good, or the chair you are sitting on does not feel good, then this choice will not be good or will not feel good if you go ahead.

Step 8: Now you get to use your head for what it is truly meant for: *asking questions* (not answering them or making decisions).

Ask "the chair" questions and allow yourself to receive or sense the answers from the chair.

You might ask questions to gain greater clarity, such as:

- Will this also feel good for others (holidaying with me)?
- Is the weather going to be favourable at this time of the year?
- Will I like it here?

- *Is there anything I need to know?* (A question good to ask every time.)

You may not get an answer in the form of words; however, you may get a feeling, image, or sense. Remember this *is* also an answer.

If you have trouble connecting or stilling your mind, a few breaths and a hand on the heart and belly may help to reconnect.

Step 9: When you have what you needed, or have a good sense from this chair, select the next chair. Sit on it and repeat steps 7 and 8 for each chair until you are all done, you have what you need, or you feel you have "the one."

Step 10: When you feel you have the option/decision, unfold the piece of paper, or open the envelope and check what it is. (E.g., Tasmania, Thailand, or Other?)

Notice how you feel upon reading the option, as it is also important information. Do you feel elated, relieved, disappointed, upset, or wrong? If you have bias or preconditioning, then you may want to override it (which you are also free to do if it really does not feel aligned).

- If you feel aligned with the right option, you have confirmation.
- If you feel disappointed, why do you feel disappointed about this option?
- If it's not what you hoped for, what where you hoping for and why?
- Is this really what *you* want to do? Are you doing it to please someone else?
- Are you attached to a particular outcome or specific way?
- Were you hoping for a different result? If so, it may help to inquire as to why. Is it valid or distracting?

- If it feels wrong, where do you sense the *wrong* is coming from? Your head, heart, or gut?
  - If it feels wrong in your head (thinking or ego), then you may want to feel into it longer or ask more questions.
  - If it feels wrong in your heart or gut, remember that right or wrong, it is an opportunity to learn to trust your senses more.
  - Why does it feel wrong?
  - What would feel right? Why?
- If your piece of paper is "other" feel into whether you need to reframe your questioning or, rethink your options, including those you may have dismissed.

You may want to:

- Reconsider the whole thing and do the chairs again at another time.
- If others are impacted by the decision, you may want to get them to do the chairs also and see if everyone is aligned with the same option.
- Write the options in a different way; for example if they have too much on them and you wrote "Camping trip to Toowoomba with friends" and "Bus trip to Timbuktu to stay with family," you might be better to consider the type of holiday, destination, and other options as separate inquiries, since a camping trip to Timbuktu with friends while visiting family may be better aligned.

Step 11: Clear the space and container that you have just made by saying thank you to the chairs and energies involved. Feel into whether it may also be advantageous to burn the paper.

Variations and additional notes:

- If you want to consult the chairs and do not have paper and pen, you could ask someone to allocate an option to each chair instead. This is done by silently allocating an option to each chair and then placing their hands on the allotted chair and silently stating the option to the chair, such as "I allocate <option> to this chair." Repeat for each chair and option.
- If other people are impacted or involved, have them sit in every chair and see if all come to the same decision.

This is a great exercise if you get too much into your head, make pro/con lists, try to think answers, flip flop, or have difficulty getting clarity or clear choices, especially if you find thinking does not help you reach right decisions.

It may seem like a lengthy and complex exercise; however, it is very simple and quick with practice. As you learn to trust the process you can simply "sit on it" and follow what feels good.

Words Have Enormous Power

Throughout this book, you are invited to take the time to feel the impact of words on your body and what feels aligned. First, though, a bit of background on why such a simple exercise is so powerfully effective.

As already mentioned, if we reduce anything in this Universe (including ourselves) down to its smallest or simplest component, it is simply energy (atomic particles moving in space). In our physical world of matter (and what matters to us), *everything is energy (light and data) and consciousness (awareness).*

Whether it has a physical form or not—things, thoughts, actions, words—all in one form or another at its core is *energy and consciousness.* When considering energy, we also need to consider power. Whether we realise it or not, when we relate and respond through action or words, we are engaging in energetic exchanges and negotiations of power. We are essentially asking: will saying or doing this empower or disempower me?

When we speak or write words, we add our own energy, meaning and consciousness to them. We become cocreators. Words are the *power* behind prayer, affirmations, incantations, mantras, magic, spells, song, and story.

The mind is programmed by thought and words. Similar to how Google mines our search history to place advertisements in our browser according to what we have been searching for, so, too, our minds have a Google equivalent called the reticular activating system (RAS), which determines what we see and what comes into our conscious awareness.

The mind takes in a lot of information, and we would be overwhelmed if we had to register it all consciously. The RAS operates a bit like a search engine, showing us the things we are searching for or what we are talking, feeling, or relating to in our lives.

This focus becomes our reality. It's why we may not have seen, heard, or noticed something until we bring it to our conscious mind, and then suddenly we see it everywhere, and everyone is talking about it. For example, we may not notice a certain type of car until we buy one, and then they are everywhere. They have always been there; the RAS had just been filtering out what it is now allowing in.

It is important to become mindful of what you say, the words you speak, and how it feels to say them, because it programs and influences what you attract into your life. We attract what matches vibrationally.

Realigning Exercise: Words

Take a moment to think or say aloud the following words while noticing *how* they feel and *where* you feel them in your body:

Bad	good	well
tired	energised	
corporation	organisation	
separation	oneness	
attuned	indifferent	

If you reply "not bad" when asked "How are you?" I invite you to test how it actually feels to say "not bad" versus "good" or "well, thanks." Even "not as well as I would like" or "getting better" is a higher frequency reply that can be used if you feel less than well and would like to provide an honest but higher vibrational reply.

Play with it. Make up your own. Find your own higher vibe replies that feel right for you.

This may sound overly simplistic, and you may think this change will not make much difference, but remember it is the small, seemingly insignificant things done consistently that have the greatest influence and effect. Thoughts and actions done regularly have cumulative benefit (or detriment) and will make the biggest difference in your life. There is great power in small things done often. Change the vibration of your words and you can change what vibrates into your life.

The Joyous Story

Words have power and put together can form powerful spells, especially when repeated. Stories thus also have enormous power and one of the simplest ways to change your life and circumstances is to change the story you tell or retell about yourself.

Today we are getting better at talking about feelings, wounds, taboo subjects, and airing our dirty laundry. However, it is not healthy when we become identified with them and make them the story of who we are, or use them as crutches rather than catalysts.

Our wounds have become a way to gain intimacy and connection, almost like a form of currency. It seems to be more acceptable to share wounds, pain, and suffering than love and joy. Unfortunately, love and joy is often not received well; it is as if we are in competition, and it make others feel worse about themselves or their situation. We even compete with our wounds, i.e., mine is worse than yours.

We are hesitant in sharing joyfulness with others as, like media headlines, we tell stories to capture the attention of others to shock, impact, or sell our viewpoints, and we sell ourselves out in the process by telling a story that does not embrace our magnificence and power.

Most of us have been raised, educated, and indoctrinated within a system based on competition and comparison, which attempts to motivate through fear of punishment, loss, or pain...as it is easier to control another when they are in fear and feeling disempowered. To control someone who is truly joyous is like herding cats—they go where they want to.

Many motivations we have learned and accepted are not our own. They help fulfil someone else's purpose. Is this why so many feel lost? A life out of alignment with your own true purpose can be a joyless one.

- Are you living your own life or someone else's?
- Are you living or being lived?

We are told to trust people and things outside ourselves like our parents, older siblings, teachers, peers, authorities, governments, institutions, and systems. We only have to look at where we are today to see they are failing us.

Things are changing quickly right now, and although traditional media and education may actively undermine our trust in ourselves, we must learn to listen to ourselves: our gut, intuition, inner guidance, authority, heart, senses, spirit, soul, whatever the most trusted inner source is for you and begin to tell a different story from a more positive and empowered perspective.

Could you rewrite the story of who you are—one that is truthfully kind, loving, gentle and compassionate with yourself and others? Where all happens *for* you, not *to* you. Write yourself a story that orchestrates a life of lessons learned and challenges overcome. Give yourself a hand and create your own joyous story.

Realigning Exercise: You as the Hero

Our need for stories is coded in our genes. We are naturally aligned with the story of the hero and the fairy-tale, happily-ever-after ending.

Most Hollywood movie plots use the formula of the hero's journey, and we keep coming back for good conquering evil, with all things working out, being resolved for and ending happily ever after. When the plot deviates from this formula we can leave feeling dissatisfied.

You can script your own empowering heroic plotline and become the biggest star in your own life. Tell the story of your life that is really worthy of who you are.

Here is a template to help get the story started. Fill in the blanks of the hero's journey.

At the start, I was wounded by _____ and battled with my _____(e.g., shadow aspect, victim archetype, weakness, or addiction) and overcame the limitations of_____ (this challenge, weakness) and surrendered to _____ (what was controlling my life or behaviours) to find my true _____ (strength, power) before I awakened to my _____ (superpower, talent, skill, gift).

To help build your story, look at what you say and whether it applies to another area of your life, where common sayings can be interpreted or associated with more than one thing. You might say you are "sick and tired of work" and wonder why you are sick or always tired. Or say you "can't get moving on a project" and complain about having sore legs. We are often telling the story of our ails and what is causing them but are not registering or listening to it.

For this exercise, we are looking to see things from a different and/or more empowering perspective. Same facts, different meaning. Most addictions actually hide wounding, so let's start there and look at some examples as the base from which to build the hero/heroine story.

- Alcohol is commonly called *spirits* and is often used to preserve things. There is *Holy Spirit* (I find it curious that alcohol was often made by monks) or *spirits*, as in ghosts. We may look for *spirit* in the bottle or look for the sense of humour at the bottom of a bottle. We could see it from the perspective that we are actually looking for our "inner spirit" but might be "bottling it." How might you turn a quest for spirit from an external journey to an empowered inner one?

- Tobacco, a sacred plant in many indigenous cultures is also used to help connect with spirit or used to clear energies and bad spirits. We talk of smoke screens, everything going up in smoke, or smoking things out. So, you might ask what protection, mask, or screen is smoking creating? What are you hiding behind? Is there a way you can face this "weakness" you want to hide or smoke out, into a strength? How are you using the power of plant medicine to find your path and come out of the mist or haze? It is often protective, especially if sensitive to the feelings and thoughts of others: How can you feel safe to turn this sensitivity into a superpower?

- Food and drink are nourishment. If you have a challenge with these, who or what are you really feeding? What are you looking for? What are you trying to wash down, consume, swallow, or digest? What themes are specific to what is being binged (e.g., sugar and sweetness in life) or what is your personal association with that food?

- Bingeing (anything) is a feast/famine energy. It is the hole that can never be filled or trying to fill the void. It is about control, loss of control, or an attempt at self-regulation. This could be reframed in the way of taking on something too precious to not completely consume, or the seeking of deeper knowledge to such a depth you become consumed by it and cannot get enough. In your story, you could talk about how you were able to overcome or extract yourself from its immense power and the effect it had on you. As a superpower, it could be a period of time when you consumed everything or felt consumed by something or everything, and how that created a reservoir within you that you are now able to draw from.

You may have noticed a theme. Many addictions are substitutes or distractions from connecting with true spirit, whether our own inner spirit or a spirit greater than ourselves (God).

Go wild, tell a big story, be fanciful, make stuff up, and do not be afraid to embellish, use puns, similes, metaphors, personification, opposites, hyperbole, or any kind of figurative or imaginative speech. This is not a time to let facts get in the way of a good story.

You may discover a greater truth in the fantastical story than you first imagined. Write a story that makes you feel good. Turn wounds into superpowers.

An example of a story is my struggle and addiction with alcohol and cigarettes that masked the anger, which could be told as a hero's journey like this:

Fearing and struggling with unknown and unfamiliar forces stirring and arising inside her, she invited in and sought assistance from the spirits, magic potions, and smoky forces to help protect and dispel the other unfamiliar house guests that had taken up residence.

Yet with time, these invited forces seemed to take on a life and agenda of their own. They lured her deeper and deeper into the shadows and abyss, consuming her life force until she felt like an empty shell. The solution had become the problem. Feeling like she did not have command of her own life, she was helpless in her actions, becoming something she neither liked nor respected.

Feeling at a loss and out of control, she was no longer able to suppress the anger raging inside her.

Through mustering the courage to acknowledge the anger, rather than denying it, she noticed that these so-called dark and mysterious friends and protectors were afraid of her. She discovered that her internalised anger had tremendous power, which could be used in creative rather than destructive ways. Her anger was distilled to initiate changes in her life and cast out the no longer welcome or needed forces that had overtaken her life. The protectors were only protecting themselves. All along she had only been wanting to reconnect with her own spirit and magic; but had been looking in all the wrong places—looking out instead of in.

Suddenly she saw how these external forces had slowly possessed and controlled her, giving her just enough to believe she had control yet not enough to leave or evict them and keeping her light so dim she could not see her own talents, potential, and power. They hoped she would not see that they needed her more than she needed them.

As she became more familiar with and embodied her internal spirit and veiled shadowy forces, she felt the difference between these opposing forces. She did not need to rage war, but simply face them and take steps towards freeing herself from their influence. As she did, her strength and happiness grew. She found new allies within and without who supported her full-heartedly.

One delightful day, she rediscovered joy had been hiding behind the smokescreen, an ally who made her feel good regardless of what was happening, a light that shone bright and endured even when things got tough. She saw herself as she truly was, full of her own inner spirit no longer needing to hide, as her light and power was not "out there," it was in here. She was the source. The source that was not just magical, it was miraculous.

Lies and Broken Promises

We may think the lies and broken promises of others devastate us the most, and while they may hurt, we may discount or neglect to notice the devastating effect and slow erosion *our own* lies and broken promises have on our joy, confidence, and sense of self.

When you lie and break promises to yourself you diminish and destroy your *faith* in yourself. It may also be harder to trust or have faith in others, because if you cannot trust yourself, who can you trust?

Honesty and integrity are grossly undervalued today. It seems lying is normal or even expected. Telling the truth is almost actively discouraged, punished, or shamed.

From the mouths of babes, the unadulterated truth becomes tainted as we learn political correctness, politeness, and good manners. We learn to say the so-called right thing or say what others want to hear; meanwhile, the truth gets swept under the carpet. As infants, we express feelings openly until we learn we are too loud, too emotional, too much work, too big for our boots, or too much to handle.

We are constantly intuiting and sensing what is out of alignment, misaligned, or "wrong," yet when we are young and told by those in authority that "there is nothing wrong"—we believe them, making ourselves wrong in the process. Even well-meaning lies make us wrong, and slowly we learn to distrust and disconnect from our intuition and truth. All could be averted if we were told more truthfully things like, "Yes, mummy and daddy are going through a few things right now, but we are working on it, and we do not want you to worry."

We grow up so that we hardly even distinguish lies, the most damaging being the lies we tell ourselves, when we say:

- "It doesn't matter" when it does (which is really saying "I don't matter").
- "I'm fine" when we are not.
- "I don't need help" when we do.
- "No" to what we really want to say yes to.
- "Yes" when it is really a no.
- "I am ____ (add criticism or judgement here)."

When you say yes to something you do not have the energy or alignment for, you need to push, force, and will your way through. When you say no to the things that may increase your sense of fulfilment and joy, you do not get "filled up." When you make promises to yourself to do something important but keep forgetting or putting it off, and when you keep putting the needs of others before your own, your body keeps score and slowly you feel drained of joy and energy. And when this becomes habitual, it may lead to illness and disease.

As we continue to let ourselves down, our shame deepens, and our self-confidence and trust erodes. The things we do and say to stop feeling guilty or inadequate, or that cover up our deficiencies, deepen the groove of shame.

For example, we might promise ourselves to go on a diet. When we fall off the wagon, we may feel ashamed or guilty; however, if we could drop the shame and guilt and simply and honestly acknowledge and accept that we had a moment of weakness, it is easier to get back on the wagon. If we lie to ourselves, saying things like "it doesn't matter," we lose faith in our ability, fuelling feelings of inadequacy and making it harder to get back on and stay on. Remember, if you fall off the wagon—don't run yourself over with it too!

Then we may try to fill the emptiness or stuff down the guilt with food. That makes us feel even more defective. And then we convince ourselves that "one more won't hurt" when we know it will. "Just one more" we lie, then "Better not waste it", and "May as well finish the packet, so I'm not tempted later." Lie after lie and we know we are piling on the guilt, anger, and judgement for "not being strong enough."

We were feeling bad, but now we are feeling terrible and wonder why it is so hard to stay on the wagon and why we do not want to get back on it.

When we continue to distract, divert, and deny with blame, shame, and lies, we fail to see the truth that might set us free—by being more loving, gentle, and *honest* with ourselves in acknowledging why we wanted to get on and off the wagon in the first place.

Dropping the shame game requires tender loving honesty. *Real truth is loving*; it is not letting you off the hook. It is facing the situation with compassion, tenderness, courage, and forgiveness. It supports and encourages, which can be a far more motivating force.

Be lovingly accountable for your actions and what is important *to you* and *for you*. And remember, love includes the wise and honest application of two very powerful words: *yes* and *no!*

Willing and Able

There is a vast chasm between being able to do something and being willing to do it.

We may give ourselves an unnecessarily hard time because we know we are capable and have the ability to do something, yet we do not do it. We are not willing or do not have willingness to do it even though we know it will be good for us. Logic, reason, and willingness do not always see eye to eye.

Achieving something (or not) has more to do with willingness than ability. When we are unwilling to do something, it is not stubbornness or stupidity, it is because we *do not feel safe*. Compassion and awareness work better than willpower, criticism, or logic. Unwillingness usually stems from childhood experiences of feeling unsafe, and for as long as this unsafe feeling remains unnoticed and unattended to, we unconsciously resist or sabotage our efforts.

I once investigated some fears and unwillingness around losing weight. Why was I unwilling to commit and stop sabotaging my efforts? I discovered it didn't feel safe for me to have a "fit, sexy body" as it might attract unwanted attention. It might require me to set boundaries I felt uncomfortable and inadequate to maintain. I felt how as child I had been sensitive to the thoughts, intent, and energy of others, but saw how it had been trained out of me and with that losing my sense of trust in recognising who's safe and who's not. Our body uses weight and fat in many ways to protect itself and us, which is why it can be so difficult to shift, keep off, or commit to losing weight.

Realigning Exercise:
Self Honesty — Am I Willing?

Each time the question is of will... "Will _____?? Will I be able to cope? Will I be able to deliver? What will others expect or think? Will it work?

When we lack will or willingness, it is because we want to protect ourselves or keep ourselves safe.

If you find yourself struggling to stay committed to something, honestly answer some of the following:

- Are you 100 percent willing to do it?
- What are you trying to protect yourself from?
- What are your true motivations for doing it?
- Are the motivations even yours? Are you doing it for yourself or someone else?
- Do you really want or need to do this?
- Are you attempting to please or satisfy expectations of others or to fit in?
- Are you locked in a cycle of shame, fear, or guilt?
- Are you trying to prove something?
- Do you feel you are able to do what it takes?
- What might be the consequences if you followed through with it?
- Are they consequences you are willing to face or find a way around?
- Are you 100 percent willing to do it?

Without willingness, it is difficult to commit as when things get tough or difficult you need the will to see them through.

Detaching Emotions from Story

There was a time when it was noble to suffer in silence. Fortunately, social acceptance is broadening, and we can now communicate true feelings and emotions more openly.

Nothing is completely good or bad, yet some of us have fallen into the trap of repetitively telling our story and becoming enmeshed in it. As mentioned earlier, wounds and traumas have become the new form of intimacy, connection, and "I hurt more than you" competition. Telling a story is not a problem in and of itself. However, we need to look at the *way* we tell the story, the *language* and words we use to do that, and how many times we tell the story.

Telling our story is helpful in gaining awareness so we can gauge where we are and how we feel about particular people or events. It is healthy to tell our story in order to understand and recognise what needs changing to create greater peace, release, forgiveness, or love.

However, when our ego becomes attached or identified with the story, it may not be so healthy. Our stories become the explanation of who we are and the validation of why we are like we are. We can become fearful or resistant to giving up our stories as it feels like we are giving up a part of ourselves. As a result, we also hold onto the pain and suffering of those stories because they are familiar to us (like keeping an old friend who hurts our feelings just so we are not alone).

When we tell or retell a story, it triggers or reactivates any stresses, emotions, and traumas associated with that story. Our body relives and reexperiences the story as if it is happening again. Over time we may embellish the story, adding further emotion, amplifying feelings of injustice, hurt or suffering, creating more stress or trauma.

Be aware that some talk therapies can do more harm than good when the retelling of the story simply heightens or increases emotional load without cathartic release. You are deepening hurt and trauma each time you tell the story rather than liberating yourself from it. You need to learn to perceive or tell the story from a different, more empowered, perspective, or do the work it takes to no longer feel the need to tell the story at all.

In order to change perspective, tell a different story, or let go of the story altogether; it helps to reduce a story down to facts. Simple or cold, hard facts tend to trigger less emotional response or reaction, and a story can have the same facts and truth but be felt differently. It is not telling lies; it is telling the truth from a different perspective. It is worth remembering that a story is what we make the facts mean. Give the same facts to ten people and you will have ten different stories. From the same facts, you can tell it from the perspective of the disempowered victim, empowered warrior, or other archetype.

When we are more attached to our story or our pain than to our lives or our joy, we are in danger because the stories we tell about our past attract experiences in our future. We may tell stories to justify our feelings or pain or defend why we are like we are. Our egos can vehemently defend our need to be right at the expense of our need to be happy.

Divorce lawyers make millions on the desire to prove the ego is right or make the other pay for pain and suffering caused (which can never be truly satisfied through money and division of assets).

In the fight to be right, rather than the fight to be happy, the lawyers are the only winners.

The path to happiness is taking our power back, admitting our part, and taking responsibility for our feelings along with telling the story that backs that. We can tell the stories that preserve pain or stories that activate feelings of power and happiness. You can tell stories of being the victim, the hero, or the peacemaker. It's your choice. However, for as long as you are enmeshed in the bad feeling stories—the stories of hurt, misery, and comparison—your heart is not open to receiving happiness, let alone joy.

Tell the story about your life that makes you feel better about yourself.

Realigning Exercise:
Reimagine Your Story

———————————————

Before we start, I wish to acknowledge that the events, facts, and circumstances in your life feel very real, very personal, and can be life-defining. I do not wish to diminish the impact these experiences have had on your life by calling them *stories*. I use this term from the perspective that it is the meaning we give to the events in our lives that gives those events so much power in our lives, and the way we feel about these events can change over time and with new experiences when we change the meaning (or story) about these events.

The facts remain the same; however, the stories (or the meaning we assign and the way we feel about them) can change with other life experiences, and when we use our power to consciously change these meanings (and the story we tell about them), it can create powerful and palpable changes in our lives.

This exercise is a bit of a variation on the hero story exercise from earlier. Quickly jot down a few events that have shaped your life. I recommend keeping to smaller, less defining events first. Leave the bigger events for after you have tried and tested this process.

To start you off, make a list of things that others (e.g. family or friends) have said that you often recollect or have on high repeat.

Check over your list and notice if there is anywhere you are invested in the story being a particular way (where you have felt another has done you wrong or where you feel you have to be right or justified). Has this also distanced you from your happiness and joy?

Next, choose one of those events. Imagine how many alternate ways you could tell this story from different perspectives. For example, tell it from:

- another or the other's point of view,
- the heart or unconditional love's perspective,
- a forgiving perspective, i.e., what opportunity of forgiveness is the story asking?
- the hero or heroine's viewpoint,
- a factual rather than emotional perspective,
- how you would have liked things to work out, or
- how you would do it if you had to do it again.

And remember the *most important* question in all this is: Do I want to be right, or do I want to be happy?

A few quick examples to help you get started:

You can tell a story of how you were hurt by another and the many ways in which they are to blame.

Or...

You can tell the story of how you recognised and discovered your needs and desires, how you learned to recognise what is important to you, and how resourceful you were in having your needs and desires met.

You can tell your story from the aspect of your hurt, pain, and suffering.

Or...

You can tell your story from the aspect of what you discovered, the gifts you unwrapped, the untapped potential you found, or the deep love and compassion you gave yourself or others through adversity.

You can tell the devastating story of a relationship breakup.

Or...

You can tell the empowering story of how you discovered your resourcefulness, how you discovered what you could do for yourself, that you were more capable than you knew and that despite heartache, you have learned to know, appreciate, love, and trust yourself.

You can tell the story about your addictions and how they have hijacked your life.

Or...

You can tell the story of a spell you were under and the personal quest you undertook in order to find the real magic potion that reconnected you with your deeper passions and truest, miraculous self.

Joyful Evolution

In many ways, the current phase of human evolution is an involution, as we need to evolve from the inside out and go deeper within ourselves. We are being asked to go deeper and live from our hearts and intuition. We are discovering the power of living and leading our lives from our inner selves and inner experiences, rather than outer ones. We are being called to thrive, let go of suffering, and work with the energies and flow so we can experience the joy of who we truly are.

It is time to bring heaven on Earth, finding the answers and solutions from within, rather than looking outside of ourselves. This requires us to tune into how we feel and recognise our innate gifts, talents, and genius, which are uniquely different and to be shared with others.

We are living in a very privileged time of change and opportunity. Today, thanks to technology and the internet, spiritual knowledge previously reserved and only available to those closeted in the highest religious orders is now available to you and me, and anyone with access to the internet. We do not have to hermit away in caves or monasteries to gain and deepen our spiritual lives; we can do it in the course of our day or while washing the dishes.

Today we ask spiritual questions like "Who am I?" "Why am I here?" or "What is my purpose?" It is unlikely that our grandparents asked these questions or used words like *manifestation* and *creating our reality* let alone discussed them in public. We are starting to live more from the inside out, as we access more spiritual knowledge while living "real" lives in the *real* world.

As we involve ourselves with evolution and live from our hearts, connect with our intuition, and follow our truth, we become more personally empowered in manifesting and creating our dreams. As we feel our union with all and serve the whole, we will experience greater flow and joy. As we become more spiritually, community, and globally aware and focused, we will feel more connected and supported. As we make peace and stop comparing and compromising our own and others' uniqueness, we will experience greater compassion. As we disconnect from our fears, and stop competing, fighting, and being at war with others and with ourselves, we will experience greater peace and joy.

Allow yourself to be in awe and wonder of *you* as a miraculous creation of the Earth and Universe. Enjoy your involution into evolution. Change yourself and your life from the inside out and experience the rewards as your inner world work is reflected in your outer world.

An Experience of Involution-evolution

Buddhism teaches the middle path, which I interpret as the path where equal opposing or extremes meet. I see it a bit like facing two-way traffic: You might tackle it head on, try to stop it, or try to outrun it; however, if you walk down the centre between the two lanes of traffic, you can walk either direction with relative ease and go with the flow. Buddhism also teaches that suffering, pain, dissatisfaction, and discontent (or *dukka*) are due to attachment. Dukka arises on conditions and ceases when those conditions cease.

Over six weeks I had a lesson in the many ways in which extremes and attachment to stuff can cause suffering. I have moved houses many times in my life; however, not as consciously or as radically as this experience. Moving house and how it impacts me has evolved. The first series of moves could be described as "moving away." Then, the next series were "moving to" places more aligned or consciously chosen. The toughest emotionally were "moving on" out of a house and relationship. This last move might be best described as "moving through and in."

The thought of moving back to my birth state of Tasmania had been on my mind for many years; however, the timing never felt right. I asked The Universe to tell me when. Six weeks prior to moving, I woke suddenly around 3 a.m. to "Beginning of July." Then a few weeks later, the guidance was to only take what would fit in my car. This move was a lived experience of attachment and suffering. I learned how changing the inner changed the outer experience and how asking questions and for help from The Universe was way more effective than trying to work it all out or control it myself.

It takes a lot of outer (physical and mental) work to move, and it takes even more inner (emotional and spiritual) work to move well. Selling, gifting, donating, burning, and disposing of nearly all my stuff is one thing, but being happy or joyous about it is quite another.

Curiosity, presence, and acceptance became my greatest allies and transformers. The most transformative action was in simply allowing myself to feel how I felt in the moment without judgement. If I felt upset, sad, or too attached to sell, gift, donate, or trash something, I acknowledged and allowed it. Each item had the potential to be something to grieve, so I allowed myself time to cry, deny, bargain, be angry, or feel how I was feeling. It did not always make sense, so I practiced being okay that it didn't and that it also did not need to be analysed. If there was something I needed to know, it would be revealed, or it would simply pass. No need (or time) to overthink it or make it into something when it was not.

By allowing the time needed (within limits), I discovered it resulted in being able to more gracefully let go of items that weeks, days, or even just moments before I could not imagine releasing. At the beginning, I agonised over each item individually, putting them into piles mentally or physically (keep, donate, sell, and trash). What comes, what goes? Do I need it? Is it practical? Does it mean something to me? By the end, I had run out of time to be sentimental and was sweeping whole shelves straight into bags to give away.

I started with the more difficult items first—burning over eighty handwritten journals, reducing a photo collection (included photos I had carried around in a backpack for two years) from two large archive boxes to two shoe boxes, destroying negatives, donating, selling, or gifting over 160 books from my treasured library, hundreds of CDs, paintings, photos, and artwork, six separate culls of my wardrobe, and a leather couch I bought to last a lifetime.

Unexpected things also came up to be let go of, like an email account deleted and the ultimate test in detaching a wisdom tooth. Two weeks prior to my appointment every night I imagined the tooth detaching from the bone (and the bone detaching from it). The surgeon (and I) was amazed that it only took seconds to extract and came out effortlessly. The anaesthetic and the stiches took longer individually than the extraction. There is an additional bonus—no pain medication needed, and it healed quickly. We really do have more influence over our body than we realise.

Many times, I thought I did not have enough time or would not be able to dispose of, distribute or sell at a price I wanted. I discovered that by bringing myself back to the present moment, changing my mindset and watching the thoughts and stories I was telling, I could turn things around quite quickly.

My greatest attachment and concern was getting a reasonable amount of money for my expensive leather lounge. I had advertised it on social and local sites for four weeks and only had scammers. I noticed I was saying, "I can't even give it away" and "Nobody wants it." When I noticed it, I said intentionally, "There is at least one person locally who would love this couch and be happy to pay a fair and reasonable amount we are both happy with." Later that day, I had two genuine offers. I chose the one that felt good, and they offered me a price within my range. After they picked up the lounge, I received a message saying, "Thank you; it fits perfectly, and we love it."

Creating greater ease and joy in my outer life happened when I took notice and was present to what I was saying and feeling while keeping faith that I could have what I wanted when I asked for it. Theory became experience.

Being aware of what thoughts and stories I was attaching to and telling—and consciously changing these with thought and stories aligned with what I actually wanted (not what I didn't) was a game changer.

When I felt upset or disappointed with how things were going, I would ask questions (rather than make statements or affirmations), and opportunities would open up and obstacles would disappear. When I had no idea how I was going to do something I would ask The Universe, "How can this be done more easily?" or "Show me how," and help would turn up or be offered—and I accepted.

I experienced the difficulty and difference in keeping myself awake all night thinking and planning, versus the ease of asking how and allowing time to receive the answer (often in the middle of the night, which I would write down and go back to sleep).

Presence, curiosity, and allowing helped things to progress or change with greater ease and little effort. I felt more aligned with my life and choices and with what was unfolding. Obstacles became opportunities.

I feel so grateful for this opportunity in really feeling and experiencing the synchronicity and miracles that resulted from this attitude. I now truly know that this stuff works and is truly powerful. Throughout the six weeks, even when things were not going well, it still always felt like I was doing what was right for me.

On the day I drove myself and a fully packed car onto the boat to return to Tasmania, the sea was calm, and the moon was full. I thanked and said goodbye to Victoria. I thought I would be sad, but only felt peace and deep gratitude as I said goodbye to the known and sailed into the unknown.

The next day I chuckled as I drove over a bridge and the sign said "Rubicon River"—no turning back now, I have just crossed the Rubicon! As I flew to Flinders Island it was still calm, the sea was so flat you could see the reflection of the mountains in it. The vibrant and beautiful patterns of the blue sea over white sand set against bands of dark blue-green beds of seaweed were so vibrant and beautiful they brought tears to my eyes. I had not just come home to my birthplace; I had come home within myself.

Realigning Exercise:
Gaining Realignment

When things are not working out as you hoped, or you feel bad about something, do you ever actually stop to notice and acknowledge how or what you are feeling?

Think of a situation or attitude in your life that you feel bad about and that you would like to evolve or change. For example, consider the following:

- an attitude about someone or something that needs realignment;
- a story you tell about yourself often that does not sit easily with you… such as one that diminishes, denies, or denigrates your gifts, skills, or talents in some way;
- a situation you would like to handle better;
- something you hoped would work out better than it has.

How does it feel when you think of this situation?

... bad, sad, glad, overwhelmed, numb, _____, _____<insert your not good enough here>?

Are you able to simply allow yourself to feel how you feel, without changing, judging, criticising, or commenting?

If not, could you allow yourself to?

If not, do you know or get a sense of why?

If not, could you imagine or be open to the possibility you could?

If yes, what happened when you allowed yourself the time to simply feel?

Did these feelings fade, move on, or transform?

Did you start feeling better or different or gain new awareness?

What do you feel has changed within yourself?

How have you evolved?

Can you imagine or feel how this might transform or change something in your life?

In what ways do you feel you have witnessed or experienced evolution via involution?

Bringing Heaven to Earth

We are living in an exciting time of evolution where it is said we are bridging heaven to Earth. It has been described to mean many things, such as a return to peace or the Garden of Eden or that humanity will return to living in peace and harmony on Earth. We may look at the world today and think that we are far from that reality and believe we are going in the wrong direction; however, I feel assured that there is a greater plan and that light is winning and that it is also often darkest before the dawn.

We are evolving from a three-dimensional (3D) reality to a five-dimensional (5D) one. In practical terms, this means we are moving away from the 3D material world of matter and where things matter, to a 5D spiritual or higher vibrational frequency where *all* matters and that we are moving from seeing ourselves as physical beings having a spiritual experience to spiritual beings having a physical experience.

The world is speeding up and so are we. We are able to access more information and data in a moment than what our parents or grandparents could at all. What we may not realise is we are receiving, downloading, and processing enormous amounts of information (thoughts, emotions, feelings, and sensing infor-mation from others and our environment in every moment). We are evolving into more attuned, sensitive, multidimensional beings capable of receiving and processing vast amounts of information from multiple sources via all the senses and at the same time. We are like super computers.

By activating our intuitive and multidimensional gifts, we become more universally focused, which (somewhat paradoxically) is achieved by being more individually self-empowered and self-governed, with the understanding that when we change ourselves, we change the world.

The heart centre (of love and direction) and solar plexus (or gut) centre (of personal power) are driving this evolution (or involution as we are going inward rather than outward to evolve).

We are starting to evolve away from left-brain dominance and its logical mental faculties, to being directed, governed, and empowered by the right (creative) mind and the heart, gut, and emotional faculties. Scientific research is acknowledging we have three brains, not one, and that the brains of the heart and gut are more powerfully connected, receiving and transmitting more data and information than the head.

You only have to see the progress of science, medicine, health, and well-being practices in the following areas to see that evolution has already started:

- Neuroplasticity – the brain is not hardwired and can change. New neural pathways can be formed or wired through repeated action. If part of the brain is damaged, another part of the brain can learn or rewire to perform that function.
- Epigenetics – how genes can be turned on or off by lifestyle and environmental factors and can have greater influence on genetic expression and diseases than genetics itself.
- Heart health – the importance of heartrate variability and coherence in creating health, vitality, and attunement to others and how coherence is shared with others, animals, and nature.

- Gut health and the importance of gut bacteria for digestion and immunity, and how bacteria can determine weight and mood.
- Vagus nerve – the rest and digest restorative phase of our nervous system that is commonly not switched on or de-activated due to modern lifestyle, stress, trauma, and diet.
- Effects of trauma and stress in relation to injuries, accidents, and diseases—especially chronic disease and autoimmune disorder.
- Energy and energetic healing – everything is energy; we are energetic bodies more than physical ones.

It is becoming clearer through these studies that we are not *victims* to our DNA and that we are not bodies comprised of parts; we are whole and holistic beings and bodies. Indeed, we are more powerful than we have been taught to believe and have untapped abilities to change or realign our lives and health. Human DNA is *not* 98 percent junk; it is 98 percent untapped potential.

The human body is a complex organism of interconnected components and ecosystems of living organisms working together for the benefit of the whole, not just a series of parts. We need to be less germ and microbe phobic and nurture these amazing little critters, as the human body is more bacteria than human, as each cell has mitochondria (which produces energy for the cell); it is not an organelle (as I was taught in school and university); it is bacteria working symbiotically with our cells.

If we use an analogy of a computer, most humans are only running the basic operating system, not even accessing or utilising the many other applications (gifts, talents, and skills) available.

Or, if it helps, imagine the human body as its own solar system where our heart or soul is the Sun and around it each organ revolves and aligns (like the planets). In this way, it may be easier to imagine being aligned with the greater Source, and each cell and microorganism within our body is like a star in the universe. And thus, when you are aligned within your body, all the cells and microorganism are aligned with you. You are the centre and source of their universe—so love them all.

Realigning Exercise:
The Vagus Nerve

One of many reasons why food sensitivities and digestive issues may be so common today is that we do not actually digest our food properly, as we are not activating, engaging, or utilising the part of our nervous systems that actually deliver energy to this process.

The nervous system has two main systems, the sympathetic (fight and flight) nervous system (SNS) and the parasympathetic (rest and digest) nervous system (PNS).

The sympathetic nervous system's fight and flight functions are activated by stress, anxiety, worry, and fear. It delivers energy to muscles and adrenal systems so we can deflect or escape danger. It also activates the inflammatory response. In order to source energy required to keep us alive and out of danger, it draws energy away from the brain, digestive, and hormonal systems and functions of the body.

The parasympathetic nervous system connects and integrates the functions of the three minds (brain, heart, and gut) via the vagus nerve. Its function is to aid digestion and cellular restoration and to turn the inflammatory response down or off.

Modern life's "always on" and "just do" mentality means that the PNS vagus nerve functions are switched off more than on. Life's deadlines, urgency, stress, and worries (which are not actual life and death scenarios but are treated by the body as if they are) constantly engage the survival mechanisms of the sympathetic system.

It helps to know how to consciously stimulate, soothe, or switch on the parasympathetic vagus nerve in order to disengage or switch off the inflammatory, adrenalised sympathetic functions and enable us to digest food and what is happening.

Twenty simple quick and natural ways to engage the vagus nerve:

1. Slow deep belly breaths (as we breathe shallow when in fight/flight).
2. Make the exhale longer than the inhale (indicating to the body it can relax). There are many breathing techniques and rhythms; one to try is to breathe in for the count of 4, hold for 4, out for 8, hold for 4, and repeat 4-4-8-4. Or just 4 in, 8 out.
3. Exercise—Walk, jog, bike, interval, aerobics, stretching—what you *enjoy* doing.
4. Yoga, tai chi, qi gong, or similar mindful calming disciplines.
5. Lie in an L shape on your back with legs resting up against a wall.
6. Meditation (guided or unguided).
7. Mindfulness—being present to what is happening without engaging with it.
8. Sing, hum, and chant.
9. Laugh (also a natural immune booster).
10. Splash of cold water on the face, cold shower, or ice-cold drink of water.
11. Gargle water.
12. Be fully present to your body and how you are feeling without analysing or judging—simply allowing yourself to feel how you are feeling.

13. Awe and wonder (especially nature such as a sunrise or sunset).
14. Affirmations or mantras like "I am feeling calm" or "Peace."
15. Press two fingers to your lips when you are feeling stressed. Our lips are rich in parasympathetic fibres (and why kissing can feel so amazing).
16. Soothing touch or massage, even just gently stroking your own arm.
17. Place your hand on your heart or placing right hand on heart and left on belly while breathing slowly.
18. Sip relaxing, soothing, and nourishing herbal teas such as lemon balm, nettle, or camomile.
19. Epsom salt bath (also great for drawing out toxins and cleaning energies).
20. Bare feet on grass or earth (even better when it is wet).

And one more, which is my favourite:

21. Spending time in nature or with animals.

Quite simply, the vagus nerve is soothed by anything that helps you slow down, relax, refocus, and be present to your body and feelings. Drawing your attention to what is happening "in here" takes the focus away from what is happening "out there." Being embodied (in your body, not your head) enables you to respond with greater intelligence to what is happening, rather than just reacting (to goodness knows what).

Choose You

It is impossible to feel the joy of being you when you are hiding out, pretending, compromising, or attempting to be like someone else. Choose your genuine, authentic, self-governing, powerful, unique, and self-determining self. Choose the you that does not need to prove or look outside for validation.

If you want to scream in frustration, "How can I authentically be myself when I don't even know who I am in the first place?" be kind with yourself. It can be tough to know or have a real sense of who you are, because in truth you are not just one personality, you embody a multitude of archetypes essential for the variety of roles you fulfil in your lives and in any one day.

You're most likely speaking archetypes every day without realising it when you describe someone as a trendsetter, caregiver, people pleaser, hero, princess, or bully. Or when you describe people in terms of roles such as child, parent, boss, leader, conductor, driver, or king, you are speaking archetypes.

Archetypes are mythical universal patterns (or roles) that can help us understand who we are and how we work in the world. The ancient Greek and Roman gods and goddesses are possibly the most widely known and are used to symbolise energies of the planets and signs in astrology, which are also examples of archetypes.

Carl Jung's work describes twelve core archetypes: innocent, sage, explorer, outlaw, magician, hero, lover, jester, everyman, caregiver, ruler, and creator.

The Book of Changes or *I Ching*, based on Chinese philosophies, defines six archetypal profiles (of which we will be two): investigator, hermit, experimenter, networker, heretic, and role model.

In terms of self-work, archetypes help determine who you are and what roles you assume in certain situations. Who or how you see yourself may be quite different from who or how others may perceive you, as archetypes are the masks we wear.

Some singers and actors have alter egos or costumes they inhabit when performing; for shy performers, it enables them to be able to perform as they work through or via the energy of their chosen alter ego or archetype.

You can also be an archetype without fulfilling that role in actuality (such as being the child archetype while an adult), or you can have the mother or father archetypal energy without actually being a parent. Others may say that you have a mother or father energy or make an assumption that you are because you exude that energy.

Specific archetypal energies will be activated or come to the fore under certain conditions. They may be activated in the presence of, or in response to, the opposite archetype. For example, the victim archetype can be activated by (and needs) the presence of the opposing energy, such as a bully, vampire, or narcissist archetype, as it is an energetic relationship. We can also embody both archetypes, feeling a victim to our own internal bully.

It is not inauthentic to be different with different people or situations—it is necessary. We show different aspects of ourselves depending on who we are with and what energies are presenting and being activated. Those whom we know well often see our more vulnerable, raw archetypes (which are not always our nicest ones), and strangers are often shown our more well-known, guarded (or better behaved) archetypes.

Some perceive archetypes as masks that need to be removed; however, they are not all bad or inauthentic, they are simply another aspect we may use in situations to keep us safe or effective like the archetypes of professional and parent, where the professional is effective or empowering for engaging with your boss and work colleagues and the parent with your children; however, it is not appropriate to parent your boss or colleagues or be professional with your children.

The key to working with masks and archetypes is around the question of power. Is the archetype working with, or against, your sense of personal empowerment? Is it helping you to express your authenticity and personal power, or is it hindering, hiding, or hijacking it? Are you playing your archetypal roles, or are they playing you?

Knowing your core archetypal patterns is one of the many ways that can guide you in understanding yourself, your motivations, and talents and how you manage your personal power. Caroline Myss, in her archetypes book *Sacred Contracts,* outlines how we all share four key survival archetypes—the child, victim, prostitute, and saboteur. Each represents different fears, issues, and vulner-abilities and the power of where and how to connect with our self-esteem.

There are not any good and bad archetypes; they are all neutral. Each have their challenges, shadows, gifts, and powers. The prostitute archetype may be one we think we don't want or is bad; however, the prostitute's powerful questions may include the following:

- At what price are you willing to compromise (or sell) your authentic individuality or hand over your power?
- Under what conditions would you be (or are) willing to compromise your beliefs, ethics, or integrity in order to gain acceptance, fit in, do a job, or be polite?

- How much power do you lose every time you say something doesn't matter when it really does—when you break promises to yourself, don't rock the boat, want others on your side, want to seal the deal, or be polite (and dishonest) towards others or yourself?

The prostitute is a very powerful archetype in power negotiations, and we need to bring it in closer rather than keep it at arm's length. The prostitute, just like all of us, wants to be loved for who it is.

Realigning Exercise:
What Are Your Main Archetypes?

Your task if you so choose it, is to get to know your true unique self by identifying all that makes up the masterpiece that is you.

We are not here to do it all alone or do it by ourselves, so you may learn to know *you* and who you *are* through your relationships, whether those relationships are with family, peers, colleagues, work, sports, friends, acquaintances, strangers, pets, nature, spirit guides, the world, or environment. Life is not a solitary journey, and we are supported in that journey. We experience who we are through connection. As we sail though our lives, we connect to ourselves through interacting with others in relationship.

There are many ways to approach this exercise.

You might want to start with the key archetypes of Jung, the *I Ching* or Caroline Myss's *Sacred Contracts* by simply feeling which one you are drawn to, which one "pings" or stands out.

- Jung: innocent, sage, explorer, outlaw, magician, hero, lover, jester, everyman, caregiver, ruler, and creator.

- *I Ching*: investigator, hermit, experimenter, networker, heretic, and role model.
- Caroline Myss: child, victim, prostitute, and saboteur.

Or you may want to read through the list of archetypes below and feel into which ones generate an emotional response or reaction.

Take special note of any that invoke negative reactions or that you might even have a dislike for or hope that they are not yours as they, in particular, have something to show you, and they may need to be acknowledged, accepted, or brought under your wing so that you can align with their gifts. These are the ones that may be running your choices without your realising it.

Archetypes:

Actor	Drama Queen	Nature Boy/Girl	Saboteur
Addict	Dreamer	Narcissist	Sadist
Alchemist	Eternal Child	Networker	Sage
Architect	Evangelist	Nun/Monk	Samaritan
Artist	Experimenter	Olympian	Scholar
Anarchist	Explorer	Orchestrator	Scout
Boss	Facilitator	Orphan	Scribe
Beggar	Fool	Patriarch	Seer
Bully	Gambler	People pleaser	Seductress
Bureaucrat	Guard /	Pilgrim	Seeker
Caregiver	Guardian	Pioneer	Servant
Catalyst	God/Goddess	Politician	Shaman
Change agent	Gossip	Poet	Sidekick
Child	Healer /	Predator	Slave
Clown	Wounded healer	Priest /Priestess	Soldier
Companion	Heretic	Prince / Princess	Spoiler
Composer	Hermit	Politician	Storyteller
Coordinator	Historian	Prophet	Student
Connoisseur	Innocent child	Prostitute	Teacher
Control Freak	Innovator /	Provocateur	Thief
Coward	Inventor	Puppet	Tramp

Craftsperson	Investigator	Puritan	Trendsetter
Creator	Joker / Jester	Queen / King	Trickster
Crone	Judge	Rebel / Outlaw	Tyrant
Crook	Knight	Redeemer	Vampire
Damsel	Liberator	Rescuer	Victim
Detective	Lover	Revolutionary	Visionary
Dictator	Magician	Ringleader	Warrior
Diplomat	Matriarch	Role Model	Wing man/
Disciple	Martyr	Rockstar	woman
Diva	Masochist	Ruler	Wise woman/
	Mediator		man
	Midas		Witch/ Wizard
	Muse		
	Mystic		

Remember each archetype has positive traits and gifts when expressed with the higher frequencies of love. If you only associate negatively with a particular archetype, ask how you could see them more positively, or in a more enlightened or empowered way. For example:

- Victim – shows where you need to develop more self-esteem or self-responsibility.
- Diva – knows what they want and will ask for it.
- Damsel – willing to seek and receive help.
- Coward – effective at escaping personal danger.
- People pleaser – has an innate knowing of what others need and want.

Alternatively, if you only see the positive or good aspects of an archetype, you are not seeing the shadow or all the energies that any archetype possesses. For example:

- Hero – may egotistically work for attention, accolades, and praise, putting self and others in danger in order to be the hero.
- Wise man or woman – tells others what to do instead of allowing them to work it out for themselves or keep it to themselves, not sharing with those who would truly benefit.
- Rescuer – disempowers by taking away esteem gained through fighting or working it out for themselves or saving those who do not want or need saving.

The list provided here is not even the tip of the iceberg in regards to archetypes; there is a wide and extensive variety of archetypal work, personality types, and profiling tests available. Please explore further if these have piqued your interest; archetypal work is very powerful.

I personally love Caroline Myss's *Sacred Contracts*. You can find more detailed descriptions of the archetypes and traits for many of these (and more) archetypes in her blog and books. When choosing, feel into what and who resonates with you and feels aligned for and with you.

Who Are You?

You compromise your dreams not because you
fear you will fail, but because you know that to
succeed you will have to rebel against the whole
of society and its expectations of you. You fear
what you might become because you do not
know who you are.

—Richard Rudd, The Gene Keys

You are unique. There is, has never been, and never will be anybody like you. The body you are in, the parents who birthed you, your life events, the friends, enemies, and people who come in and out of your life are all part of a perfect orchestration enabling you to fulfil your unique role and purpose in this lifetime.

Whether you see yourself as a piece of the universal puzzle, a thread in life's tapestry, a part of the cosmic plan (or theatre), or a cog in the engine, when you take your place or role, you complete the puzzle, tapestry, plan, play, or engine.

When you are not being who you are, like a missing piece in the puzzle, a pulled thread in a tapestry, a cog not turning in the engine, you are not taking your place and being you, doing your thing, and things just do not work as they could.

We are powerful beyond measure. You are powerful beyond measure. It is impossible to be in this world without influencing or impacting something or someone in some way. You have a reason for being here, a role to fill that is unique and personal to you, and integral to the whole. The truth is, we have absolutely no idea of the impact we have. It is not something we can fathom. We are so intricately interwoven.

Your role does not have to be big to be important. What if your purpose was simply to be here to give someone a timely smile or encouraging word, the smile or word that changed their life and changed history? Although I trust there is more, what if my purpose was simply to write this book whether anyone reads it or not, the act of doing it may be vital to something somewhere. Seemingly small or inconsequential actions can have huge consequences when we consider the web. Change in just one person can change many, for better or worse, so let's start by being kind.

All this said, where do you find your role or reason? Where do you find your own particular version of "who am I, and why am I here?" Primarily, the answer is found in your heart. Listen to your heart, and you will find your reasons.

You might say, "How can I follow my heart when I do not trust it or when I think it has failed me?" In your heart (not your head), you will find real love, direction, and who you truly are. If you stop being entangled in the head's doubt, confusion, and having to know, you can drop into your heart. The reply you get may not be logical; however, it will make sense. You are a cocreator. Follow your heart and create the aligned creative life you desire.

Realigning Exercise: Design Your Perfect Day

Admittedly when I first came across this journaling exercise, I thought it would be a waste of time. Yet, upon starting, I discovered some very important and interesting information. First, that I had absolutely no idea of what a perfect day would look like or how I would like it to be beyond sunshine and rainbows. I did not know what I wanted or needed to create the perfect day for me. I didn't know what would make me feel successful or capable in life, even if success or capability would make it perfect, as a perfect day was more about *not doing much at all*. I discovered I had a spectrum of perfect days.

Choose a question or prompt to journal and play with it, until if feels really good and juicy for you:

- What would be your perfect day?
- Who or what do you envision being?

It helps if you can really get into the details and sensations, so that you can almost feel you can touch it. Below are some guiding questions to help get additional detail. Imagine the sensational details—how it feels to see, smell, taste, hear, and/or touch it—to be really involved in this perfect day.

- Is there anyone with you? If so, who (person or pet) and how does it feel to have them there?
- Are there specific things you would like them to say to you or anything you would like them to be doing for you?
- (If relevant) What is the weather like?
- Where are you? At home, office, holiday destination, particular location, or place?
- How do you feel physically, mentally, emotionally, and spiritually?
- How do you know it is your perfect day?
- What details make it your perfect day?

And yes, be fanciful and wild beyond what you would normally allow yourself to imagine. This is your perfect day; it goes beyond what you believe could be true. Stretch yourself and play with some ideas and really get a sense of what lights you up and makes you smile—remember it is *your* perfect day. This is not the everyday dream—this is your joyous ever after. Or if that feels like too much pressure, your joy for now and after.

Competition and Play

Critics who treat 'adult' as a term of approval, instead of as a merely descriptive term, cannot be adult themselves. To be concerned about being grown up, to admire the grown up because it is grown up, to blush at the suspicion of being childish; these things are the marks of childhood and adolescence. And in childhood and adolescence they are, in moderation, healthy symptoms. Young things ought to want to grow. But to carry on into middle life or even into early manhood this concern about being adult is a mark of really arrested development. When I was ten, I read fairy tales in secret and would have been ashamed if I had been found doing so. Now that I am fifty I read them openly. When I became a man I put away childish things, including the fear of childishness and the desire to be very grown up.

— C.S. Lewis

Great disconnect occurs when we compare ourselves or live to the expectations of others, instead of to the beat and drum of our own heart. Comparison and competition (even with ourselves) are usually driven by ego, and in the ego is not where you find joy.

Whether competition is healthy depends on motive. Are you competing to win or to play? To prove or improve? To show others you are better than them, or to better yourself? Competition can change how you feel, and the real question is, how does it change how you feel *about yourself?*

Play is where you find joy. Joy does not care if you win or lose. Play is the love and joy of doing, the feeling that arises from doing something that sings from deep within. Joy cannot be measured. Joy does not care what others think. It does not even care what *you* think. Joy plays *with* you; a celebration undefined by others.

It is through play we get to express our true genius and allow it to come to the surface. We are the most creative when we are playing—when we are in a childlike state of wonder where there are no mistakes, errors, failures, objectives, judgements, comparison, or competition. Just play. It is the following of the curiosity, following the energy, following what makes us happiest. It is when we do things for the joy and not for the things. It is when we play for the feeling, not the result.

Play may have no reason, yet it has great purpose. Make play your *greatest purpose* in life. We have become too left brained, too reasonable, serious, and logical, which cuts us off from our creativity, imagination, and true genius. Great inventions are discovered through the process of play, making mistakes, and evolving through these (so-called) failures. Play *with* and *in* life as if there are no mistakes or failures (because there aren't).

Have serious fun and play for the joy of it.

Realigning Exercise:
What Stops You from Playing?

Unfortunately, formal education and the way in which many of us have been raised does not foster or embrace true free play. Most board, card, computer, and educational games are structured towards engaging the solution-oriented, logical (left) mind with formulas, strategies, and rules to follow or obey. True play is free with few rules or restrictions, and with engaging the creative (right) mind; it is playing with the box the game came in.

Be lovingly curious and interested as to why and when you may have lost (or never had) a free creative connection with play. (This is not a time to shame or blame as that would be *being* played, rather than playing.)

As you read the list below:

Notice which statements feel true to you or invoke an emotional response (even if they make no logical sense or there are no associated memories).

Acknowledge what you are feeling and say aloud "I feel <emotion> that <statement>" e.g., "I feel angry and upset that I was never allowed to play." Honour these feelings.

If it feels soothing and comfortable: Place a hand on your forehead or over your heart or give yourself a hug or gently stroke your forearm.

Accept how you felt or are feeling without changing or adding shame, blame, guilt, or judgement. Simply witness and allow this emotion to be, and it will simply soon no longer feel this way (and you may instead feel the peace of acceptance).

- I don't know how to play.
- I was never allowed to play.
- I don't have time to play/I never had or have time to play.
- I am no good at singing/dancing/painting/drawing/writing/playing/telling stories/making stuff up (so I will not do it).
- Play is silly/stupid/useless/a waste of time.
- Games and having fun are not for me.
- It's all fun until someone gets hurt.
- When I play, bad things happen.
- I will get into trouble if I play.

- What will others think or say?
- People will tease, mock, or make fun of me or what I make.
- What if I get it wrong or make a mistake?
- I cannot do it well enough.
- I feel self-conscious.
- I feel like I am being watched.
- People will judge me as _____.
- I always lose / end up in a fight.
- I have nobody to play with.
- … any others that pop into your awareness.

Bring your power back with radical responsibility. If you think that you are not someone who plays games, I invite you to play a game of: What game are you playing now and who are you playing it with? If you are blaming someone or something as an excuse to not play, you are in fact playing an unhealthy game. Be honest with yourself. Do you see that no one is stopping you right now, except you? If you say you do not have time, how can you play with time and find five minutes to doodle, gaze, or swing on a swing?

Be lovingly honest with your reasons or excuses as to why you do not play or make the time to play. What things do you do in your day (cooking, cleaning, chores, driving to work, brushing your teeth, making a shopping list) that you could do more creatively or have more fun with?

Where do you wish you could play more? What do you wish you could play? What steps can you take right now to play?

Realigning Exercise:
Playing with Play

Play opens our hearts, minds, senses, and possibility, allowing "mistakes," experimentation, and adventure. Play connects us with the joy of following our inspiration, energy, and creative flow.

What can you do in your life more playfully?

Make a list of all the things you enjoyed and loved playing as a child, or that you wished you could have played with as a child.

When completed, book an appointment with your child-self and make it a priority. Keep it and do not let adult things distract you from playing.

If reliving your childhood does not appeal, then if you have a project (even better if it's dull or boring), consider playing with it. Imagine all the different ways you could do it. Imagine all the things you could do with it. Go for wild and wacky. Do not judge anything. Be ridiculously creative. It may help to set a timer for a few minutes to create focus.

Are there any ideas within all of that which may be good to give a go, or might make the project better? Experiment with a few ideas, affirming there are many ways and no mistakes or failures.

Other ways to play:

- Housework and cleaning can be much more fun wearing a tiara and bopping along to music that makes you feel happy. Play with it. Dress up, put on a superhero outfit, or use the vacuum, broom, or mop as a dance partner.
- If there is something you enjoy doing, could you make it more fun or creative? If you love cooking, do a Masterchef

Mystery Box Challenge—how many things or what could you cook with a particular ingredient?

- Doing just about anything to music you love is a great way to play. Let go of inhibitions and sing along like nobody is listening!
- Tell your life story as if you were a superhero.
- Doodle your emotions. Express your creativity and emotions by allowing your pen to move itself.

Realigning Exercise: Drawing Your Story

Get out your pencils, crayons, paints, or pens (or whatever you like or have) and doodle, draw, paint, or sketch three pictures.

Quickly, without editing or thinking, allow them to almost draw or paint themselves. As you finish one, immediately start on the next.

Play and let it all flow without editing or judging yet notice any thoughts and feelings that arise. If you feel intense emotions coming up, simply allow yourself to feel what you are feeling. Do not analyse, change, or fix them; feel and allow the emotions to move through you.

When you have finished all three, place them in the order they were done and look at the three together.

Now you get to play some more. Create a story that connects all three as past, present, and future.

If it helps, you can use the following prompts to help create your story:

1. In the recent past I have been feeling _____.
2. I now feel _____.

3. In the future I want to feel _____.

Is there a pattern or theme that plays out in your life or situations?

The Ego

We often find it challenging or difficult to make time to play as the ego might say it is childish, a waste of time, or is not something someone our age (or shoe size) should do. The ego (as you may have found in the previous exercises) can be too serious and controlling to allow play, asking any variety of why, how, and what-if questions. Questions are actually better asked and answered through play and discovery, which is part of what play is all about. Too often, however, we think we have to know it all and have it all planned out before we begin, killing creativity before it has even started.

So, what is the ego? There are many answers, although the way I see it, the ego is mainly concerned with separation and the soul is concerned with unity. The ego operates through the mind and the soul through the heart.

The ego (often called the small self) can get a bit of a bad rap and make us think we would be better off without it, or that we at least need to beat it into submission. As much as the ego will have us comparing ourselves to others and making ourselves feel better or worse about ourselves, the ego is also important. Yes, it can cause a lot of grief; however, you are invited to accept, acknowledge, and befriend the ego—to work with it, and have it work for you—rather than keep wrangling and fighting it.

As humans living in a physical reality, we essentially require an ego; at its essence, I see it as what keeps us in human form (or separate) from all other energies. It can be perceived as the structure holding us in physical form in a physical body on this Earth so that we are not just energy flying everywhere. It separates us from Source (and may be why *ego* is perceived as negative).

If we were to become completely egoless, we would lose the ability to exist in a physical body. To become truly enlightened is to no longer identify with the ego and to return to Source, to no longer be earthbound in a physical body with earthly interactions.

To make the most of our earthly experience and work with our ego, we need to awaken to it and not be a victim. In other words, we need to have our ego working for us, rather than us working for it. Love the ego, yet do not be *in love* with it.

When our head or conditioning dictates our life, we are being ruled by ego. When we follow our inner authority (our heart, gut, or intuitive senses), we are being ruled by our soul or spirit.

We can listen to the ego; however, we do not have to do as it says. Our ego is not best equipped to run the show—our spiritual self is much better connected to guide us. (Something the ego will *not* be happy to hear.)

The ego has many tricks for manipulating us. It is the ego that will fight to defend a stance to be right, to relive past hurts, to use guilt or shame, and to have us avoiding the present or facing our shadows. As we get to know our egos better, we can live freer, more joyous lives through a truer connection to unity than separateness. Put the ego in the back seat, put on the kiddie locks, and do not even let it play with the windows or the radio.

The ego may convince us it can make us happy; however, it cannot show us the path of joy, as joy is beyond ego. The ego's gift is in showing us where we can grow, learn, and realign.

Realigning Exercise:
How Healthy Is Your Ego?

Time for an ego check: Is it healthy or is it not?

Unhealthy Ego	Healthy Ego
Do you:	Do you:
• *think* (rather than intuit) what is best for you?	• intuit or have deep knowing of what is best for you and follow internal guidance, even if illogical?
• override your intuition if you think it is irrational?	
• know what is going wrong for or what is best for others and can't wait to tell them (whether they want to know or not)?	• intuit or know what is going wrong and what is best for others *and only share if or when asked?*
• tell everyone how good you are in an attempt to hide or distract from your lack of confidence?	• feel quietly confident in your own abilities and live by example?
• feel the need to prove or always be or get it right?	• feel your confidence is not diminished if you make a mistake or are wrong and are willing to learn, change, or correct if needed?
• have an unwillingness to learn, change, or correct if you are wrong?	• accept that mistakes happen and take responsibility for them without shame?
• deny and feel shame when you make a mistake or deflect it by blaming others?	• feel humbly proud of what you do and do not need to seek validation, yet

• feel falsely proud of what you do, with a deep need for others to validate you? • deflect, diminish, or not fully receive compliments by saying things like "what, this old thing?" or "it's nothing"? • think in terms of "look at me and how great I am," or alternately "don't look, I'm not good enough." • loathe or say you love your physical or mental aspects, yet do not actually appreciate them?	appreciate it when received? • accept you (and others) for who, what, and how they are? • feel inherently good and good enough? • graciously receive compliments with a "thank you" or simple acknowledgment? • think in terms of "see me, or not, it does not matter. I am enough." • love, appreciate, and accept the physical and mental aspects of self and how they work for and with you.
Does your language or thoughts go in the way of: • It happened TO me. • The world owes me. • I am entitled to this. • I am uniquely special, living on this Earth at this time, to do something special and be someone special. • I need to save the Earth / world.	Does your language or thoughts go in the way of: • It happened FOR me. • The world does not owe me. • I am entitled to nothing, yet abundant by birthright. • I am uniquely individual living on this Earth at this time. I only need to be authentically myself and live an honest life.

• There is nothing I can do to help the Earth and it does not matter what I do as am only one person / the Earth is here for me to use as I deem fit. I am spiritually awake and anyone who does not wake up and take this path is <insert judgement here>.	• The Earth does not need saving; however, I do make a difference when I act responsibly, ethically, and sustainably and when I am kind and caring of myself, others, and the environment. I choose to live a spiritually awakened life and respect the path and choice of those who do not.

Part III

Realigning Heart

One way to be less adversely impacted by the egoic or small self is to live less in and from the head and live more aligned with our true, great, soul self by living aligned with the heart.

Much of my life, I lived from my head and egoic self, which was exhausting as it kept telling me the many ways in which I did not measure up, was not good enough, and had to do more to be a better person. It would also tell me how others did not measure up, or how they were not good enough, so I could feel a little bit better about myself.

I have experienced major burnout at least three times in my life. Each burnout was the result of different reasons (being too much in my head, feeling inadequate, trying to prove myself, having to get it perfect or forcing, controlling, or pushing with willpower); however, despite the reason (or excuse), the common denominator was that I was living out of alignment and not listening to the guidance of my heart. I was listening to everything and everyone outside and not having the faith to trust my own intuition or guidance.

It helps to remember there is no degree of difficulty in miracles—big or small—they are all the same in the eyes of The Universe. The role of the mind in miracles is simply to ask for it and notice it when it happens, not to "make it happen." Between the asking and the receiving is the alignment of universe and heart. It helps to remember that if you are experiencing fear or feel you are not being enough, you are in your head (ego) rather than connected and aligned with the power of your heart and intuition that knows what your mind does not.

Joy resides in the heart (among other places). By living from your heart, following your heart's desires, and feeling the love in your heart, you can feel more connected with your joy. The heart is a path to joy. By opening your heart and being heart-focused, you can experience more joy and the rewards of an open heart can come in many surprising ways.

We have been conditioned to believe that if we close our heart, we will be protected and not get hurt, yet the opposite is true. When we close our heart, we also shut out the experience of awe and wonder. The heart has its own wisdom and protection and knows things the mind cannot.

Paradoxically, a closed heart does not protect you from hurt, although the mind may think it does. If you have ever been side-swiped and hurt by someone's decision to end a relationship, you may have been in your head and not listening to your heart. Your heart knows when another's heart is not in it, and it is able to read beyond words and actions as the heart contains enormous wisdom.

An open heart (even if it is hurting) is open to receiving love and healing—a closed heart is not. An open heart will heal, and it will hurt again, whereas a closed heart is stuck in hurt. An open, aligned heart guides you to the best outcome for both. Unrequited love is not truly love, as to truly love you must be able to allow it to be free.

It is possible to end a relationship in love. A relationship ended in love provides incredible healing and transformation for both. Yes, once again, it may still be sad and hurt, yet there is an undercurrent of joy, purpose, or the knowing it is not to be. You may feel sad it is over yet maintain a sense of joy. You may acknowledge it was not as you hoped yet be joyous for newfound freedom. The end of a marriage or relationship does not have to mean the end of friendly relationship.

When I ended my last relationship, it was because of love. The love was not lacking, it had simply changed. My heart knew that as much as we loved, appreciated, and respected each other, I could not be who he wanted me to be, and he could not be who I wanted him to be. Doubting my decision many times, I would need to check in with my heart and ask, "Have I done the best thing for both of us?" (it always told me yes). Or if I was tempted to call him for help as I had learned to rely on him, I would ask my heart, "If he asked would I be prepared to get back with him?" (to which the reply was no, so I would stop taking the easy way out and source help from elsewhere).

By questioning the integrity of my actions, I stopped myself from being cruel to myself and him. I used to worry that I had done the wrong thing by him and cried from joy not sadness when he confirmed he was much happier in and with his new relationship than he was with me. Our relationship was for the purpose of personal growth, and we were great for each other once upon a time, yet happily ever after together was not to be.

Aligning Your Heart

Our hearts have an energetic field that is felt by others and that attracts things that are a vibrational match into our lives. The greater capacity we have to feel love and joy, the greater capacity we have to be open to receiving that which brings more love and joy into our lives. Like attracts like.

To realign our capacity to receive more love and joy in our lives, there are eight powerful ways to help align the heart.

This is through the **eight powers** of:

- "I am"
- Story
- Trust
- Loving your body
- Gratitude
- Compassion and sharing
- Loving Self
- Choice

The Power of "I AM"

"I AM" is a powerful statement and incredibly creative energy of self-expression that speaks to and from the creative source of The Universe.

When we make the statement of "I AM" we are declaring ourselves as cocreators with God, which is a birthright, not blasphemous or deserving of punishment. We are all Suns (not sons) of God. "I AM WHO I AM" is a statement that says: No matter when or where, God is there.

DNA is changed by "I AM," so it is wise to be conscious and careful with what else you attribute with *I am* statements. Remember that words have power and that words used in specific sequences create spells. Each time we repeat those words we recast and strengthen the spell. (Advertising and news are actually forms of spell casting.) I invite you to stop here and reread this paragraph to really allow this information to land.

Using "I am" statements inappropriately diminishes our power, such as when we say things like "I am sad" or "I am happy." Feelings are *not* who we are. Feelings are simply a cocktail of chemical reactions moving through the body. Feelings are fleeting. Saying that feelings or emotions are who *we* are, does not empower us, nor does it make us feel confident, safe, or stable since they are highly changeable and inconsistent. As mentioned in part I, they may not even be ours.

It can help to share our feelings with others, rather than keeping them to ourselves. When sharing, be aware of the greater truths. Try saying, "I am *feeling* sad" or "I am *feeling* happy" rather than "I *am* sad," which makes an emotion your identity and disempowers you.

Powerful "I am" statements are things like I am love, I am joyous, I am powerful. (Remember: love, joy, and power are states, not emotions.)

Realigning Exercise: Affirmations

Affirming the following "I am" statements regularly can help activate personal power and creative potential, as they calibrate your heart, direction, and self-expression.

I am joy.

I am loved, loving, and lovable.

I am compassionate.

I am free to choose and decide.

I am divinely supported.

I am energy, vital and alive.

I am forgiven, and I forgive.

I serve; I am served.

You may want to post these somewhere prominent where you'll see them every day, such as on your mirror.

Also, remember our purpose is about *be*-ing, not *do*-ing.

Living, breathing, and loving are our purpose. The things we do are expressions of who we are; they are not our purpose.

The Power of Story

Storytelling is a powerful part of life and society in indigenous cultures. Stories share the history and wisdom of peoples and ancestors. They tell of where they came from, who they were in the world, and how they lived, survived, and thrived, which helps us all align with our own story. Story is an integral part of spiritual practice and tribal connection and is not restricted to the spoken word. It is conveyed through all forms of expression (dance, art, crafts, living, work, etc.).

There is enormous creative potential and power in telling our story. And the most fascinating is the one we tell *ourselves!* What we say about ourselves and to ourselves through our inner dialogue says a lot. So too do the tales we tell about ourselves to others. They all have impact on our energetic and physical bodies. Many stories we tell about ourselves are through a lens of adversity or trauma, and whether we are aware of it or not, we are all entangled because human history is traumatic.

Trauma may be a result of our own experiences (individual trauma), carried through genetics, family stories, beliefs, or programming (ancestral trauma), or social, cultural, racial, religious, community, or worldviews (collective trauma). Regardless of the source, it can keep us stuck causing us to repeat or escalate patterns or it can give us an opportunity to heal.

Often viewed in a negative or disempowering light, trauma is also the story of survival. Many definitions are restrictive, resulting in thinking that it is reserved for war veterans, horrific accidents, or victims of crime or abuse. This narrow view undervalues the impact our own life experiences can have on our sense of who we are and how accumulated childhood experiences and happenings (although not traumatic at the time) can become the foundation of post-traumatic stress (PTS) and also autoimmune, chronic, and mental illnesses.

Trauma is a very complex topic and not something I can do justice to in a chapter, let alone in a few paragraphs; however, it needs inclusion as the tendrilous nature of unresolved trauma and its reactions can adversely impact relationships, finances, work, creativity—everything really—physically, mentally, emotionally, and spiritually. It is insidious as it can hijack our personality, compromise our vitality and sense of safety, self-esteem, health, self-care, and thus also our joy. It is also often hidden or at the base of the stories that we tell and the ones we may tell on high repeat, whether directly related to the trauma or not.

An important thing to understand about trauma is that it is not what happened (the event or situation) that creates the trauma—it is what it meant. In other words, it is the story that gets entangled with what happened.

In some tribal cultures, if someone is deeply traumatised, they will be called into a circle to be witnessed in telling their story in its vulnerable entirety three times (and no more) and after which they are to never tell the story from the victimised perspective again. They believe if told more than three times it "becomes them" or takes their soul.

Some very important things to highlight:

- It is important to not let "the story" become your identity and way of engaging with the world.
- There is powerful healing in holy witnessing or listening (the silent honouring and witnessing of another and their story).

- Sharing a story can heal or entrap (depending on perspective).

We are at a stage in human evolution that is asking us to address and heal our traumas so that we can become more open, loving, and joyous beings. Trauma is not just caused by a "big" event, there is also constant or accumulative effects of "little" (possibly unregistered) events that may be even more insidious in impacting behaviour, choices, and the way we feel about ourselves. The stories we tell about these events can either further entangle us or can help release us.

One way to notice where individual, ancestral, or collective trauma may be resurfacing is to notice the voice of the inner critic or the victim and what stories they are telling. Learn to not berate or ignore it; instead, congratulate yourself each time you notice it. From here, you can notice the pattern and change the inner critical message to a less fearful and more compassionate one. A message that is a loving and encouraging message from your inner loving self, inner loving parent, or inner loving team, whichever message needs to be heard or recognised.

We can be terrible at recognising our own needs, so listen to the needs underneath what you say so you can work towards getting your needs met.

Although somewhat oversimplified, our story essentially aligns and attracts into our reality situations, people, and events that support it. Stories full of drama, heartache, and chaos are more likely to attract even more drama, heartache, and chaos, giving you more of these stories that you love to tell.

If drama, trauma, and heartache are not what you want to dominate your life, tell it differently such as how you overcame challenges, the lessons you learned, and how you took responsibility and ownership for what has happened so that joy, empowerment, and well-being can be gleaned from these experiences.

To make something clear, please do not think that if you only tell "good" stories that "bad" things will never happen or that it means you are doing something wrong or out of alignment. Life is not a flat line; it is a wave, with ups and downs. It has variability. Life is not static. Loss, failures, and storms happen; it all depends on how we move through them. With an open, aligned heart, you will be able to navigate life better and circumstances may impact you less. You may still get hurt; however, you may not get flattened or traumatised by it.

The greatest gift you can give yourself is the story of forgiveness, as *forgiveness breaks patterns*. If events and situations keep repeating or playing out, we have to truly forgive: forgive others, forgive God, forgive ourselves, forgive being human.

View your so-called mistakes, errors, sins, faults, and major eff-ups simply as experiences or exercises in learning greater acceptance, compassion, love, tenderness, gentleness, and forgiveness.

My Realigning Story: Healing Trauma and PTS

While working in a call centre the headset had been turned up to full volume by another accidently. I took a call and was unable to turn it down in the usual manner, resulting in acoustic shock. Although intensely unpleasant, it was not what caused the trauma and PTS.

The trauma (and then the PTS) was first caused by the lack of concern and support of supervisors or those I thought *should* care because it was part of their job description. Being dismissed and told to go back and finish the last hour of my shift certainly contributed.

The obstructive and challenging attitude of the Work Cover Manager and the ever-changing requirements, forms, interviews, appointments, and hoops that had to be jumped through in order to be *so-called* supported by the system caused considerable stress and the trauma escalated. Fortunately, the doctors, who were actually the ones I thought I might need to convince, were wonderfully supportive and saw things were not well even though it was not a visible injury, and they too were having issues with this particular Work Cover Manager, which helped in me thinking it was not just me.

From this personal experience with PTS and Work Cover, I discovered that while I was still blaming others and getting entangled in the drama and story of what they did *to* me or did not do *for* me, I was not going to get better. *Plus*, to be covered and supported by Work Cover means you need to remain injured. And the objective of Work Cover is to return you to your previous role, which I did not want to do. This meant there was going to be very little incentive for me to get better.

Things changed once I recognised the true underlying trauma was that *I did not keep myself safe.* When I took complete responsibility for the whole situation and stopped blaming others, my condition improved. When I forgave myself and others—seeing them as people who were helping me make a decision I was too scared to make (leave a job that I neither liked nor suited me)—things improved further.

The feelings of injustice niggled for longer. I thought about making a complaint but realised that even if I won, it would change little for me or others, as they did not believe they needed to change anything and just saw me as a troublemaker.

The sanity preserver and decider was the question, "Do I want to be right, or do I want to be happy?"

I kept choosing *happy*. Fighting was not going to make me happy. It was going to be a bold move, as I had nothing to go to, was still recovering and running low on funds. However, my guidance kept urging me to have faith and trust and so I followed through and quit my job and Work Cover. And The Universe supported me in ways I had not imagined or planned; the acoustic shock, PTS, and self-esteem improved.

There are still some side effects such as voices in close proximity being more difficult to hear than those further away or over background noises; however, I no longer go into states of anxiety or panic over loud noises and am able to use earphones or earbuds without meltdown.

The turning point was taking back my power and taking the responsibility for not keeping myself safe. Disentangling myself from the drama and story with the realisation that justice and fairness is not always what we think it is. And most importantly, I had to forgive myself. No longer was I telling the victim story and thus no longer feeling angry or worked up about the injustices every time it was told.

I had freedom to choose happiness and healing and there is not one day that I regret that choice. When I changed the story, I healed, aligned, and changed my life.

Realigning Exercise:
Your Realigning Story

Choose a writing or journaling exercise that aligns with you:

- Is there a story you tell that makes you feel entangled each time you tell it?
  I.e., does telling a particular story make you emotionally triggered or angry, worked up, loud, animated, or raise your blood pressure or heart rate?
- Is there a situation or event you would like to disentangle from?

What could change in this story that might help you disentangle from it?

- Do you have a story that you would like to rewrite or tell in a more empowering way? (Like changing perspective from victim to empowered....)
- What lessons or experiences have you had that could be shared that might help others to navigate their lives more powerfully or easily?
- What discoveries and adventures (or misadventures) could you tell about what you learned or how you would do it differently next time (not that you need a *next time*)?

Now, work through any of the above with the formula below:

1. **Notice** the trigger, core theme, or sticking point in the story that you are telling. (What activates the most emotion?)
2. **Acknowledge** how it truly makes you feel or where you could take greater ownership of what happened. Where are you losing power and where can you take it back?
3. **Accept** (as difficult it might be) that it did happened, and that you can no longer wish to be negatively impacted by it. Accept that there is something you need to do or let go of.
4. **Change** the story or change the perspective from which you view the story–such as walking in others' shoes or changing the angle from which you view the story. How can you take radical responsibility and change the story you tell?
5. **Forgive** who you need to forgive. Or where do you need to forgive yourself for not doing what (with hindsight) you would have done at the time?
6. **Imagine** how the story could be retold so that you reclaim your power and esteem or imagine how you would like the story to unfold.

The Power of Trust

A trusting person or soul is a more joyful and loving one. A trusting soul feels greater freedom to play and dances with the flow of life.

The main reason why we distrust ourselves is that we have been taught to give our minds too much power. Our minds are not actually designed to make decisions and answer questions! (More on that later).

We need to relearn to trust our hearts and guts as the true sources of wisdom and guidance. The mind has information and knowledge; however, it is the body that has wisdom.

Self-trust is possibly the most underrated yet most important thing to develop. After all, if we do not trust ourselves, who can we trust or how can we know who to trust? In this information (and misinformation) age, we may have discovered we cannot trust certain organisations, institutions, systems, and even governments that we thought we could. We may have also had experiences where we felt let down by an individual or group we thought we could rely on or trust.

Not everyone deserves our trust, yet we need to trust in something and in someone. This is why we need to trust ourselves first and foremost, so we will know who or what we can and cannot trust out there.

Trust, intuition, and confidence are like three points of a triangle. Each supporting, feeding, and leading to the other. In the middle is faith. Strengthen one and you strengthen all.

When you trust your intuition, your confidence grows. As your confidence grows, it is easier to trust your intuition and the more intuitive you become. As you allow and trust your intuition to successfully guide and navigate you through life, you get to enjoy life more.

Trusting in a spirit or higher informing or guiding force or source requires us to be connected with and to trust in our intuition. Connect with what feels good, loving, and all-knowing as it helps to feel we are part of the greater good, and of purposeful service. Being able to place our faith or trust in something greater than ourselves and feel a grace-filled loving force has our back and is able to support us when we ask allows us to rest. Even though what we ask for may not always come in the package we hoped, it comes in the way best for us to learn and grow, although we may not recognise it at the time.

We need to spend (a lot) less time thinking and more time feeling and sensing. We need to *go out of our minds and come to our senses!*

Learn to trust your heart and solar plexus (gut) for guidance, wisdom, messages, and timing. Although we may perceive the Source as being outside of us, it is actually found deep inside our body. Go within, or you may go without.

Trust in life is like a beautiful dance. It's about being in the right place at the right time with the right people supporting you in the next right step. An orchestration of events that play out harmoniously be**for**e you (that they *be for* you).

Realigning Exercise:
Universe "To-Do" List

You do not have to do everything yourself. Ask for and allow yourself to receive help and support.

If you use or like to-do lists, make sure you have at least two columns. One that is yours to do and one that is for your trusted divine loving supportive source to do (insert your reference to God, Universe, or Divine Source).

My to do	God/The Universe to do
• Ask for help for what I cannot do myself. • Ask The Universe to take care of the *hows*. • Allow myself to receive support. • Ask God/Universe to help me to source the inspiration, courage, energy, and alignment needed. • Ask to be guided in what I need to know. • Be open and available to respond and make the most of opportunities. • Be intuitively open and receptive.	• Support me (which it always does). • Take care of the *hows*. • Provide divine grace and energetic support. • Help connect with my inspiration, courage, energy, or alignment to do it. • Guide me. • Send clear messages to respond to, creating greater ease and flow in my life.
What else can I *ask* for assistance, help, or support with? What actions do I need to take care of myself?	What else can The Universe help me with? What plans do I have that I need help in aligning all the stars?

Realigning Exercise:
Trust to Faith

Trust or faith in anything can only be achieved when you have trust and faith in yourself, and it starts with being true to your word.

Developing your faith and trust is very simple. Set yourself up for success. Start with something that is easily manageable or something that you may have been procrastinating over and decide to do it every day for a week.

You might choose to:

- Be in bed by or before 10:00 p.m. every night.
- Walk around the block every day.
- Cook a healthy meal every day.
- Smile and give yourself a wink in the mirror every morning.

It does not matter what it is; you just need to do as you say—no excuses!

By the end of the week, you should be feeling better or pretty good about yourself. Yay, that is what we are after.

You feel good because seeds of true self-esteem and confidence are growing, as is your faith and trust.

When you trust yourself, you can hear the quiet voice within that guides you (your intuition) and have the faith to follow it.

Something as simple as trusting and keeping your word can create a mountain of faith that reduces the mountain of procrastination into the molehill that it is.

The Power of Loving Your Body

Possibly the greatest joy we can experience is the joy of the human body. Yet why is loving and appreciating our amazing, sensuous, miraculous, wondrous, sexy, juicy, shapely, wise, _____ body such a challenge?

We hear supermodels and Olympians say they do not love their bodies. Maybe, like me, you wonder how this can be possible. People can feel betrayed by their bodies in many ways and capacities.

Much media harms and damages the way we view our bodies, mainly due to comparison. Photoshopped images are well-known to be damaging. Yet, few people stop to consider the possibly even-more-harmful body image that results from science, medicine, and even alternative therapies, which sell us the message that unless we are well, we have failed in some way, or our body is betraying us.

One example is the way in which we talk about autoimmune disease. We are told it is the result of our body attacking itself. Why would the body attack itself? It may make more sense that *autoimmune* is our body showing us the many ways in which we attack ourselves through our thoughts, criticisms, judgements, comparisons, and choices.

There is also the possibility that autoimmune is actually our body *protecting* us from or against something. What if it is something not easily found unless science was actually looking for it, like a virus, toxicity, or accumulations in our body reaching levels too high? Our body works relentlessly towards creating health, so is it addressing something unseen or unknown?

In order to have the vitality we wish to have in life, we need to care for and care about our bodies. Even though we are energetic and spiritual beings, our earthly experience is one of embodiment, an existence in a physical body.

Comparison and body-shaming are rife. The main reason is that we believe and allow other people's judgement, criticism, or opinions to override the truth of our bodies. We do not see our bodies for what they truly are and what they are really for.

What is the truth about your body? Your body is purpose-built for what you are here to accomplish. Your body is the perfect vehicle to take you through your life and accomplish all you are here to do or be. Forget the designer clothes! They are still mass market. Your body is one of a kind, the most specifically designed outfit, down to the finest specification and detail. Your body is designed for *your* life and lifetime.

Feel the joyful power of your words in your body. Say aloud: *"I love my amazing body! My body brings me joy."*

Realigning Exercise:
Body Appreciation

We are bombarded constantly with images of how beautiful bodies should look; however, do we truly see *real* bodies? And I am not just talking about photoshopped images, I am also talking about how we do not truly see our own bodies as they really are. We may obsess about what we do not like or how we would like it to be different.

The objective of this exercise is to see your body in a different light and find different ways you can appreciate it, so you can take greater care of this incredible miraculous and amazing vehicle we know as a human body.

Looking at yourself naked in a full-length mirror may be confronting to start off with; however, the objective is to get to the stage where you are able to see yourself full frontal and at least appreciate what you see, even if you cannot love what you see, yet.

The first thing to unlearn is that a perfect body fits within certain measurements. There is no measure of beauty and beautiful bodies come in and are all shapes and sizes.

The aim of this exercise is to focus and look at a part of your body that you appreciate, like, or love and to expand this focus until you can include the whole body.

You can start with an elbow, ankle, foot, leg, breast, shoulder, chest, eyelash, scar, or any part from a specific angle—it does not matter—just look at this part either directly or in the mirror.

Allow yourself to feel the appreciation or love in your heart for this part of your body.

Then gradually move your focus to extend a little further out from that part or spot.

Notice any thoughts (negative or positive), judgements, or criticisms that arise as your focus expands and as you undertake this exercise. Simply notice without pushing the thoughts away or giving them more thought. Maintain a soft and loving focus.

Then ask, "Is it true?" and **feel the answer in your heart.**

If you say, "Is it true my ankles are cankles/fugly/fat/_____?" or whatever it is you believe. Do not think or analyse. FEEL IT and feel how it feels to be untrue.

If you feel it is true, ask, "How could I learn to appreciate or love this part of my body?"

The objective of this exercise is to generate appreciation, acceptance, and love. I do acknowledge this may be an incredibly challenging exercise; however, persevere and start small and work up as this can be incredibly transforming and any work that you do to increase your appreciation and love of your body is work well worth doing.

The idea is to work up to the stage where you are able to look at yourself naked in a full-length mirror and accept, appreciate, like, and even love what you see. Although you will be physically looking with your eyes, look from the heart, not the head.

The Power of Gratitude

The power of gratitude is underrated, often being negated as airy-fairy stuff; however, gratitude is a very powerful way to change your life.

Gratitude opens our hearts to receiving life. A heart full of gratitude is also full of joy. An open, grateful heart receives support from others. A person with a grateful and open heart allows others to support them and supports others in healthy ways.

Gratitude is not just a solid foundation for manifesting and attracting more of what we want in life; it's a way to align more deeply with our life and emotions.

When we live a life of gratitude, grateful for the very breath that sustains us and the very life force that lives within us, we set ourselves up for experiencing more joy in our lives.

A state of gratitude tones and works the receiving "muscles." When we express gratitude *before* we have received, it sends a strong message of faith and trust—two essential components in working cocreatively with The Universe.

The Universe supports us when we express gratitude for what we receive and the many ways in which we receive it. Be open to receiving unconditional abundance—allow yourself to feel gratitude for this universal loving source.

There are many simple and easy everyday ways you can increase gratitude and the magic that it can create in your life.

Realigning Exercise:
Not Happening *to* Me — Happening *for* Me

―――――――――――〜〜―――――――――――

If you can stop thinking things are happening *to* you and instead look for, acknowledge, and say thanks for the many ways that life works, colludes, and happens FOR you, you may find a deeper appreciation and gratitude for things in your life.

Looking from the perspective of *for* enables you to tune into the many ways in which life is synchronous and gracious towards you and is working *for* you. It becomes possible to see how "bad" things can be or actually are *for* your greater good if you explore the possibility.

It may require hindsight or time for the benefits to be seen; however, the truth is that life colludes more *for* you than against you. For example, as I look back, there were many times I was upset by something, such as missing out on another job; however, most times there was later the relief and gratitude of dodging a bullet.

Write your story about what events you have, or can, reframe from happening *to* to happening *for* you.

Realigning Exercise:
Finding Good from Bad

―――――――――――〜〜―――――――――――

Gratitude may be experienced as a result of the unlikeliest of events and prove to be a magical force.

A friend described the loss of her sweet husband to cancer as a life-changing and crushing loss, as she misses him every day, yet without losing him, she said she would not know if she would have ever learned to live so fully and joyfully. She feels she may have stayed stuck in the mundane and not have pushed through walls to truly *choose* life. She is thankful for him and the love he showed her every day. She is grateful for the way that through her love for him, and how much it hurt to lose him, she gets to see the world in a vibrating emotional resonance that she could not have imagined before.

What crushing events have you experienced in your lifetime? Where have you, or can you, find good in the bad? The pearl in the oyster?

Realigning Exercise:
I Am Grateful For

Give life to your gratitude by speaking it out loud: "*I am grateful for...*"

In my twenties and thirties when I felt consistently depressed, apathetic, and just plain *blah*, it was not surprising to discover I was ungrateful for life and for my life. It was surprising in my fifties to discover I was still not grateful for this life despite feeling much happier within myself and my life.

It is challenging to truly tap into the joy of life without being connected to the feelings of gratitude for life and for being here on Earth at this time.

Without expectation or judgement, ask:

"Am I grateful for life?"

"Am I grateful for my life?"

Regardless of your answer, allow yourself to feel it for a few minutes and allow yourself to acknowledge what you are feeling.

After a while, you may feel a shift. Only once you have felt this, and if your answer was no, find at least three ways in which you can find gratitude for your life. If you are having trouble, feel the gratitude for the people, pets, or places that you love.

Realigning Exercise:
Gratitude for Your Body

This truly miraculous and amazing body that we reside in and experience our lives through is something we may take for granted or actively loathe.

If you find yourself feeling ungrateful for your body, try looking at your body with childlike wonder, curiosity, and play; be fascinated by your body. Wonder about how from just two tiny cells you got this body, head, arms, legs, organs, skin, nails, fingers, and toes.

Look at your hand. Move your hand and see how your hand, thumb, and fingers move. Connect with what might be required to coordinate all the muscles, ligaments, bones, and nerves to move. Wonder about how just the thought of moving your hand can make it move. Wonder at how it also moves without even thinking about it.

Your body is truly amazing; immerse yourself in the wonder of your body and the many things it does to not just keep you alive, but also to keep you happy and joyous—if you get out of your own way.

The Power of Compassion and Sharing

Possibly the most accessible path to opening and activating the heart is through compassion, sharing the joy of who we are and the joy of who they are.

Fundamentally, we are designed to share, be of service, and cooperate. Our own bodies are a vast network of trillions of cells and microbiome that instruct, interact, cooperate, and share resources with each other. Each cell in our body performs specific and specialised tasks, and in doing so, they are nourished and supported by other cells also doing their specific specialised tasks.

Specialisation (or uniqueness) achieves far greater efficiency and possibility when done in cooperation with and supported by the whole rather than an individual cell doing it all or doing it only for or by themselves.

Taking this to the human level, when individuals do the tasks they are specialised in, proficient at, and love performing, stronger, more highly evolved communities result. This is the direction human evolution is heading – greater appreciation for the individual and their gifts and talents, for all to benefit from and enjoy.

Sharing is the energy of compassion and service. When we generously share our gifts and contributions with the world, it not only serves us; it serves the whole, the greater good of all and the planet. Giving with compassion and service is a clean exchange of energy.

Being aware of what we are feeling before, during, and after sharing gives valuable information in regard to the energy being engaged. For example: If you find you are resisting sharing your knowledge or gifts, is it because you fear another may take or get advantage over you? It is vital information, yet dig deeper. Is this energy telling you it is your fear, or their intention? If it's your fear, are you able to realign with love so you feel free to share if appropriate? Or are you picking up on their intention to take advantage rather than receive, recognise, and honour what you have to share? It is all about energy and the objective is to keep the energy neutral or clear.

Discernment in sharing helps create clear and neutral energy exchange. It feels amazing to share when we are invited, recognised, or received honourably. It is not as great for us to share when others do not appreciate or want it (takers and non-receivers) or when we share in an egoic way in order to prove, force, or push coming from a place of lack, rather than abundance.

Being of service is sharing, not giving what you do not have to give. If you do not fill your own cup first or have good self-care, you will have less, little, or nothing to share. You drain your own energy resources and become a drain on the resources of others, including those you think you are serving.

If you are being of service or sharing out of duty, with resentment, or to get something in return, you are neither sharing nor being of service. You are shortchanging others and yourself. You are cutting them off from being able to receive fully and cutting yourself off from the source of return.

Be aware that return is not necessarily direct, it may be paid forward via other people or means, *and* it is returned tenfold. It may not come right away, yet it does come. Remain receptive to receiving in every moment so it does not back up and so you do not have to receive flat out when it comes.

I used *back up* and *flat out* very intentionally, as the spine (back) represents support. The spine (or back) can give out or give in when we back away from giving or receiving support; or when we are inflexible or less upstanding in the balance of sharing. If we are too busy giving but are unwilling or unable to receive what is coming back, it is possible that we may end up with little choice but to receive being flat out sick in bed or hospital.

Knowing when to share, give, or receive…and when to not is a powerful thing. There is great power in giving generously and receiving graciously; however, the greatest power is knowing when to NOT use your power (and especially when you really, really want to).

It helps to discern when you are using power over or power with. We all feel the pressure to share at times; however, first stop and ask: Is this truly helpful? Do I think I know or can do better than them (power-over)? Or, can I wait to be invited or asked to share what I know or can do, which may enable them to find a better way (power with)?

We may lack generosity in sharing as humanity broadly has a tendency to believe we need to hold something back in reserve whether due to fear, lack mentality, or aversion to risk.

Many think we need to work hard to get ahead, and see the world as an unfair, unjust, tough, dog-eat-dog world; however, when we truly see the true nature of nature, we will see the many ways in which we live in a generously abundant world. Nature is not actually about survival of the fittest and competition, it is an intricate and intimate **co-operative** system where ecosystems are interwoven, feeding and supporting one another.

Great and generous gifts do not have to cost you—a smile, a kind word, encouragement, love, patience, compassion, understanding (especially at the right time!) can be life-changing.

Do not underestimate the impact simple acts of kindness can make. A warm, compassionate smile or word can be a beacon in the darkness and can even save a life. (Thank you to the unknown stranger who passed me on the street with a smile so bright it lit the deepest darkness.)

Compassion and sharing improves our resilience, makes us healthier, and allows joy to bubble up from deep within.

Realigning Exercise: How Do You Truly Feel About Sharing?

With the attitude of "there is no right or wrong, there is only information," notice what feelings or thoughts come up for you when you say aloud:

I am compassionate, and I share my gifts and talents with those who appreciate and recognise them.

Without thinking or analysing, simply notice and allow what comes up to come up. Without trying to change or fix, simply acknowledge what arises upon each inquiry:

- Was it easy and comfortable to say this statement aloud?
- Did you feel your energy expand or contract?
- Were there any parts that felt difficult to say aloud? If so, which bits?
- Were there any words or parts that you stumbled over, choked on, or felt uneasy saying? If so, which bit(s)?
- Are there any particular words or parts that resonate?
- Are there any particular words or parts that feel discordant?
- Which parts feel expansive/bigger or contracted/smaller?

- Did any thoughts, images, or memories arise from reading this statement?
- What parts felt true and which parts did not? Do you have any sense of why?

Place your hand on your heart, take a few deep breaths and say the statement aloud and earnestly two more times allowing time for the statement and words to settle into your blood, body, and bones.

How does saying the statement aloud now feel different from when you first said it?

The Power of Loving Self

Why is saying someone loves themself rarely said as a compliment? Ironically, this is often directed at people who do not love themselves but are overcompensating and hoping to convince others of the many reasons why *they* should love them, as they do not truly love themselves.

Self-love and self-care are not just bubble baths, spas, retreats, and weekends away. Yes, those are wonderful things to do as part of self-care, but they are not going to dramatically improve your self-love if you spend your time criticising your body, feeling bad about yourself, or leaving it until you are so sore, tired, or wired that you are forced to do something.

If your self-talk is depreciative or you are criticising others in order to feel better about yourself, you are neither in self-love nor self-care.

Judging, criticising, or being derogatory about another is an indication you do not truly love yourself. Once again it is a time to look at your egoic thoughts, conditioning, and beliefs and question that which has made you question your love and acceptance of yourself and who and how you are.

With aware parenting today (thank goodness), more children are being raised with greater acceptance of who they are so that they can grow up with a greater sense of self-love.

No need to despair if you were not raised by aware parents or in this manner; *you can raise yourself* in that manner now.

One of the most loving acts you can give yourself is self-parenting, which is something you can give yourself in every and any moment (when you remember to!). Self-parenting is simply saying to yourself loving, tender, compassionate, and encouraging words and placing loving limits that care for what you need *now*. It is repairing and providing a different story for those moments of hurt that are still active (and triggering) from childhood.

For example, if you are going through a tough time and feeling fearful of moving forward, instead of telling yourself to "buck up," "get over it," "stop being stupid," or calling yourself a "scaredy-cat," or whatever your version is, instead, offer words of validation and encouragement like...

I hear you and see you. I am sorry things are feeling a little rough or tough right now and that you do not really know which way to go. (Validate whatever is going on for you.)

I have faith in you. You always seem to be able to work things out. (Offer words of encouragement that you need to hear.)

Even if it does not feel like you know the answers right now, they will come. You have done well, and I am so proud of you and all that you have done. (Tell yourself what you need to hear.)

Be aware that if you were not raised with encouraging language or not used to talking or being talked to in this manner, it is going to feel incredibly false, uncomfortable, and awkward. It will feel like a foreign language, but I promise you it is worth working through the discomfort and awkwardness. Allow yourself the time to learn and expand this new language of self-love.

You may try it a few times and dismiss it as stupid or pointless. It is okay to drop it, but please pick it up again. It may fall butter side down, and you may need to wipe the floor, but three-second rule! Dust it off and take another bite. Please be gentle with yourself, but please also give yourself the encouragement and the loving limits so that you also persist. You cannot truly love another nor allow another to love you until you love yourself.

True self-love is not showy. You do not need to convince anyone. It is simply a no nonsense, no apologies, *"This is me. Trust you like it, as I am not going to turn myself inside out to be more acceptable to you."*

It is about saying, *"I am not for everyone and that is okay, as I accept myself for who I am. I do not need everyone to like or love me, as many already do love and like me as I am. I love, accept, and appreciate my own uniqueness and the uniqueness of others. I am unapologetically myself and if we are aligned, I would love you to join me."*

Realigning Exercise:
Change Your Self-talk

If you want to change the way you feel about yourself, it helps to start with changing the way you talk to and about yourself. To feel more loving about and towards yourself, you need to talk more lovingly to and about yourself.

Swap out any unloving, blaming, shaming, critical, or conditional words for embracing words of encouragement, support, validation, acceptance, and unconditional love.

Whenever you say something to or about yourself that does not feel aligned or congruent with your loving, expansive self, say three things that are. You do not have to say them aloud, although saying them aloud adds power to your words.

Speak to yourself in the manner and words of love and encouragement that your inner child (and current adult) wants and needs to hear to feel loved, cherished, and valued.

I hear you and I get it. How can you speak in a supportive, loving language when you have not been raised with the vocabulary?

We may know the words or language (and threats) that make us good, keep us in line, or toughen us up; however, supportive, loving, or encouraging words may have been thinly dispersed.

Kind and encouraging words may feel very uncomfortable or even repelling if they have been used as weapons to guilt, shame, control, or manipulate you. Allow yourself to feel and be curious with what you are feeling when you use these words so that you are informed with the information, healing, and realignment they can provide.

When I first came across this reprogramming or re-parenting of self, I did not even know what words were supportive or encouraging. I would say things I thought were but be shocked when someone would say, "Gee you are hard on yourself." I wondered what they would have thought if I said what I used to say.

This work takes learning a whole new vocabulary and language (I am still learning). From my own experience and experimentation, I can affirm that even the smallest of improvements can make a huge difference in building confidence, esteem, and how you generally feel about yourself. Start before you are ready to. Start now! Say something encouraging, even if for the moment it is just saying genuinely to yourself, "I've got this" or "I can do this." What a fantastic start!

If you are up for a bit more of a challenge, say compassionately aloud:

I love me. I love who I am. What a joy to be me. It feels joyous to be me.

Realigning Exercise:
Love Letter to Self

Write a love letter to yourself, outlining all the things you appreciate and love about yourself.

You may either create a list of attributes you appreciate or would like to appreciate and accept about yourself.

Alternately, you may expand on them and really feel into how they help you. Even more powerful, see if you can expand some of your (so-called) weaknesses and see their strengths.

Dear <your name>,

I love and appreciate _____.

Example - List:

I love and appreciate your empathy for others, organisational skills, logical and scientific mind, creativity, resourcefulness, thriftiness (or stinginess), acceptance of others, openness, sensitivity, faith, alignment with truth, patience, hyper-focus, listening skills, drive for improvement, integrity, endurance, passion, aptitude, adventurous nature, experimental, imagination, thirst for knowledge and truth, wisdom, wonder, desire for knowledge, ability to integrate many concepts, and so much more.

Example – Expansion:

I love and appreciate your resourcefulness and creativity as it enabled you to keep yourself safe in situations requiring quick thinking and new solutions. It has enabled you to be successful in management and coordinating roles and careers and enabled you to achieve the impossible. When money was scarce it enabled you to feel rich, as you have not missed out, as you have been able to create what you wanted for yourself from what was available.

Example – Weaknesses into strengths:

I love and appreciate your stinginess, as it has recruited your resourcefulness and creativity in new ways. You have created many things simply from the wonder of whether you could do it. Your stinginess has opened and expanded your experimental, adventurous, and wondering ways and enabled you to create and care for yourself in ways you may not have otherwise. It has reconnected you with the joy of creating, just because you could.

I love and appreciate your sensitivity as it enables you to tune into the needs and feelings of others, which enables you to relate with them in a deeper and more intimate way.

I love and appreciate your lack of confidence, as it has enabled you to understand what it is like to have it and not have it. It has enabled you to be empathic towards others and why they may sabotage their dreams, aspirations, and selves. It has provided wisdom through experience of what builds true confidence and what does not.

The Power of Choice

Have you truly recognised that you can decide to love yourself more?

It seems strange and also amazing that there are things we think we know, yet on reflection discover that we did not actually know it. Some things are so obvious, they are obscured or visibly invisible, in plain sight yet not seen. I feel that choice is one such thing; it seems so obvious, yet we do not fully unlock the power of choice, as we forget to choose the power of choice.

Making a choice is incredibly powerful, as it sets an intention which ripples out into the cosmos and returns with the means to manifest that choice.

What makes the earthly experience so unique in this universe is that we have free will and freedom to choose. Thus, *the* most disempowering feeling we can experience is the feeling that we have no choice. Truthfully, we always have choice, even if it is the choice not to choose.

Many spiritual teachers say that we have no choice and that "Thy will is my will"; however, even in this case there has been a choice. The choice would be to give up your choice to choose your own path. It is the choice to follow God's directive and guidance instead of making your own choices along the way. Even if you follow that path, there is always the choice to step off it or to no longer choose that path.

The simplest and greatest empowering choice comes from the wise and deliberate application of two very simple words: *yes* and *no*.

It is important to say no to others crossing your boundaries, treating you disrespectfully, abusing your good nature, or taking you for granted, or to say no to yourself if you disrespect your own values.

Saying no to putting yourself down, dimming your light, continually putting others' needs before your own, or making any hurtful, judgemental, critical, or "joking" remark about yourself or others gives you great power.

Saying yes to compassionate, loving treatment and commentary and getting needs met healthily is critical. Learn to say yes to receiving these things from yourself, not just from others. Everyone deserves kindness, compassion, and love.

You get to choose the empowered words of your story and decide what opportunities you take. Choose and decide what connects you to joy.

You know the drill; say aloud:

> "I choose."

> "I decide."

> "I get to choose and decide what's best and aligned for me."

We Always Have Choice?

I believe it is not what we do that is the most important, it is that we are *aligned* with and consciously make the choice.

In my mid-forties, I experienced health issues and consulted a number of medical professionals. (Unfortunately, or fortunately) I seemed to find a series of medical practitioners who used shock and fear as tactics to achieve compliance and have me do what they advised me to do. Some appointments left me in such shock that all questions escaped me. Contradicting advice and concern between specialists and doctors became confusing, so I decided to do my own research to gain greater understanding.

I was prescribed a "new-generation" blood-thinning drug, which I questioned because the whole reason I started seeing the doctors was because of anaemia due to losing too much blood. (I had bled nearly every day for over a year, sometimes profusely.)

The doctor did not seem to understand my concern and was visibly shaking as she held out the script and with panic in her voice advised, "You have no choice, if you do not take this you will die."

I looked at the script, then locked eyes with her and said with more courage than I felt: "We always have choice."

She trembled as she shook the script at me again, and as I took the script from her trembling hand (to make *her* feel better), I had a vision of bleeding to death.

When I was nearly out the door, she called me back. "I have to tell you. There is no antidote for this drug. If you bleed, you will bleed out. Vitamin K does not work for this drug." I cannot remember if she also said "you will bleed out and you could die" although it is the message I heard. I had replaced *could* with *will*.

Although my "vision" was compelling enough, I like to do my research. So, I checked it out on Drugs.com and other websites before disregarding it completely. There it was: *Side effects: Death!* "Fatal bleeding was adjudicated death with the primary cause of death from bleeding. Very common (10% or more): Any bleeding (up to 28.3%)."[1]

---

[1] https://www.drugs.com/sfx/xarelto-side-effects.html#refs

And "make sure you tell the doctor if you have bleeding problems." *Ummm... I am sure they have an extensive recorded history. Why are they prescribing this particular drug; do they want to kill me?*

I felt I was at far greater risk of death from this drug than my condition (deep vein thrombosis, which the imaging doctor doing the scan had not been overly concerned about, having not whisked me straight to hospital, which is what they advised would happen if they were alarmed).

I also knew things the doctors never asked about: I had just ended a significant relationship, had been depressed and sedentary, had been spending way too much time sitting on my new (grief purchase) leather couch. I had also been eating a lot of parsley to up my iron levels (which unknown to me prior, also aids blood coagulation).

I thought about following advice and making a tombstone with "I told you it would kill me," but decided instead to live or die on my own terms and choices. I chose to trust my intuition.

Maybe a different blood thinner would have been more suitable, but I actually did not want to take any medications on offer. I needed to do something, so I made cayenne pepper balls rolled in coconut oil.

I am not going to pretend it was a walk in the park. There were many sleepless and anxious nights, waking moments filled with dread and doubt as to whether I had made the right choice. I got better at checking in with my body and my own guidance, asking, "Am I going to be okay? Is this choice still correct and aligned for me?" The answers remained *yes* and *yes,* and as time passed, so did the anxiety.

The next scan showed great improvement, the clot was dissolving and had not moved or broken off. The herbs, regular exercise, change of diet, and therapy were working.

Out of curiosity about a year later, I re-researched the drug to see if anything had changed or if it had been taken off the market. An article on a reputable site stated that an estimated 90,000 people in the US are admitted to hospital each year because of uncontrollable bleeding and that the FDA were investigating faulty clinical trials.

The greatest gift of this experience was learning to trust myself and my choices. WOW, I had to make hard choices. Thank goodness I also had the courage, conviction, and rebellious spirit to go against advice many would not even question. I can love myself for that if nothing else.

I love that I did not buy into the fear nor follow the advice or agenda of another that did not feel aligned for me, just because they had letters after their name, or I thought they knew better than me. I love that I chose to trust and back my choice and that I trusted myself with my own life.

Realigning Exercise:
Aligned Choice

We do not all make empowered and aligned choices in the same manner or with the same process.

Do you know what is the best way for you to make choices and decisions?

Most people make the best choices and decisions emotionally or via the gut. You might notice that thinking or using the head or mind is not listed. We rarely make good choices by thinking or making pro-con lists. How many times have you made a list and then gone against it anyway?

Before you proceed and find your way from the list below, first think back to a choice or decision that:

- Turned out well and still feels good today. And what was your process in making that decision and following it?

And also one that:

- Didn't turn out as well as you hoped, or that felt good at the time but didn't deliver. What was your process in making that and following it?

Work from your experience, using the list for confirmation and clarity, rather than informing you. You may not recognise your best aligned decision process at first as you could be using the correct method incorrectly. For example, if you make best decisions emotionally, however are executing them while in an emotional state without allowing time to gain neutrality and clarity, you will not be getting best results. Similarly, if your process is via gut response, but you are being pressured with too many choices, you will be unable to discern which is the best choice.

Do you recognise your way of making the best aligned choices or decisions?

- **Emotionally** (50 percent) - allowing time (at least sleeping on it) to feel into and notice how you feel emotionally about a choice over time and knowing the aligned choice is one that feels consistently good despite changing mood or situations. If you feel differently, or your choice changes or fluctuates with mood or situations, then this choice is not as aligned. You may also find that quick, instinctive choices do not work well for you. The bigger the choice, the longer the time required. Your choice is most aligned when it feels neutral (not emotionally attached). Be patient and follow your feelings.

- **Fluidly/flow or gut response** (30 percent) – allowing time to feel a gut-like pulse that indicates how you feel. It may feel like a gut response or attraction/repulsion or expansive/contracting indicating a yes/no choice. You may find you gain greater clarity in choice when asked specific questions with a single or yes/no answer. You may find that multiple choice can confuse your ability to make a single choice. Follow your flow and gut.

- **Instinctually or spontaneously** (10 percent) – feel instantly and instinctively what choice is correct and aligned. It is easy to miss or doubt and you may change your mind as you go along (know this is not being flaky; this is correct and aligned for you). Follow your instincts.

- **Wilfully or whole heartedly** (6 percent) – making choices aligned with your heart and what you want. (It may feel a bit egotistical, yet you may discover what is right for you, is also right for others.) Follow your will. When you do something against your heartfelt will, the energy is mis-aligned and likely to cause issues or problems at that time or later.

- **Vocally** (2 percent) – as you talk to another about your choice you gain greater clarity of whether and which choice is aligned and correct for you, as it sounds right or resonates with you as you talk about it. You may find that you prefer talking with people who are better sounding boards. Follow your voice.

- **Lunar/month** (1 percent) – it takes a long time to make important choices as you need the time (and all phases of the moon) to truly know how YOU feel (rather than how others feel) about this decision or choice. You may feel guilty about it taking such a long time to make decisions; however, you also know that it is needed. Follow your voice over a lunar cycle.

- **Clarity or just knowing** (1 percent) – clarity about decisions suddenly arise or come through external signs or intuition. You need to be careful to not think, overthink, or think the head has the answer. This is the clarity of knowing what choice needs to be made. Follow your clarity.

Which way of making aligned choices is yours?

Part IV

Realigning Your Creative Self

Genius is our most precious and innate gift which is accessed through creativity. Genius is unique and an expression of our uniqueness. Life is not designed to be a prison. It is designed for the creative expression of our heart through our actions and the beauty of who we are. When we do not know who we are or have lost connection with the beauty of what we love, we can feel stuck with little or no energy or enthusiasm.

If you feel stuck, you have lost connection with your purpose, dreams, and aspirations. If you find yourself bored with the every-day tasks (eating, cooking, cleaning), seeing them only as chores, you have lost connection with your purpose. Purpose sees chores as vital steps that keep you healthy and enable you to do what you love and love who you are.

When you are being true to your purpose, *all* things have meaning.

Purpose runs underneath our daily acts and activities. Each task we undertake—even dusting and dishes—can carry the energy of beauty and can feel purposeful and effortless.

If you are stuck or confused about your purpose, start with love. Express all forms of love. Make whatever you do an extension of your beauty. Live, breathe, love, and allow joy.

Realigning Exercise:
Love to Play

I get it. Simply saying to start with love, breathe love, or allow joy sounds like platitudes not practicalities. It's simple to say, yet not so easy to do.

I believe the main reason we have lost connection to what we love and love doing is because we have lost our connection with play. We have been taught to take things too seriously, to think about our futures and be responsible for things outside of us (like super-annuation and retirement plans even before we start working), rather than attend to the things inside of us. We have not been taught to discover and attend to the richness that exists inside of us, which takes care of the future because the only place we can change our future is in the present moment—in the NOW.

Play allows us to be present; it is the adventure that takes us inside ourselves. We get to express our inner beauty and genius through play. Creative play is not just about art, song, music, dance, writing, inventions, or crafts, it is also about movement, ideas, and experimentation; it is doing something differently or doing it our way. We get to express and play with our expression to create something that is truly ours and makes our hearts sing (though actual singing is not required).

Play is allowing what needs to come out and be expressed to simply be expressed in the way that is needed. It is not about creating masterpieces, or bestsellers, although that may be a fortunate result.

Play is formless; it is not right or wrong or something to be graded or assessed. Play is for the sake of playing, for the joy of expressing, for allowing your childlike wonder to be exercised.

Find your love of play. Find *how* you love to play and *what* you love to play with. Start with what you used to love doing as a child.

Self-alignment

Healing is realigning. The process of healing is, in fact, the process of your body, cells, and energies realigning to find harmony. Our bodies and lives are in a constant state of flux; we are continuously changing and responding to happenings within and surrounding us. The infinitesimal changes may push or pull us out of alignment, requiring us to regain, retain, or realign with a new centre of alignment, even if just for a moment, as the (so-called) line (or goal posts) we are aligning with are also constantly changing.

Let's find the magic potion within ourselves. Our bodies are already using every measure to maintain alignment in a world where we are told on every billboard, publication, and station the many ways we are not good enough and inadequate. We are brainwashed to believe we will miss out if we do not buy, have, or follow such-and-such.

It is difficult to be joyful when we are attempting to align our lives according to the values or beliefs of others, rather than our own. Self-alignment requires finding your own way and path of your true genius and gifts.

Truth and integrity are pivotal in alignment. We may do our all to keep a promise to another yet break promises to ourselves without a thought. If you have ever said, "It does not matter," when it does, you have come out of alignment.

Realigning Me

It is said that our activation to heal (or realign) usually begins with intense emotional reactions, such as sadness or anger. For me, it was many emotions; however, anger was the predominant one and it was a horse that both showed me I needed realigning and how to do it... and for a while it was a question of who was going to kill who. A horse could do what no person could and teach me what no person could teach—patience and unconditional love.

My realignment involved getting out of alignment and being thrown headfirst into a horse float and landing on the tow ball. I count myself lucky that essentially all I ended up with was a haematoma in my right butt cheek the size of a half-deflated football.

The lesson or opportunity from this accident was the realisation I had to stop listening to what everyone else was telling me to do and start listening to what felt aligned. It also involved learning to listen to what my horse was telling me and asking of me.

This started a process of becoming more in tune with not only my horse, but also with myself and my environment, which also helped me source assistance from people and qualified prac-titioners that I felt aligned with for what I needed.

Realignment required looking at my childhood, and although there were many painful memories and many things I could not previously remember, I can say from experience that the pain of suppressing and holding it down or keeping it in, is way worse than the fear of letting it out or admitting it. In time, over-whelming fear transformed into relief.

I found a few practitioners I trusted and made great progress with and some I only worked with once. Unafraid to try and even experiment in finding the right people or techniques for me, I was loyal to myself and my healing, not to a practitioner or method. I worked with who and what worked best and felt aligned for me at the time.

With the workplace injury and PTS, I realised that "the systems" do not work well for me. Although imperceivable that Work Cover would be so trauma uninformed, it did lead me to my own research. The pivotal lesson for me was the realisation that I had to take responsibility—I had not done all I could do to prevent my injury. There was little point in blaming others, or the system. If I was going to get better, *I* had to get better.

I have made many radical decisions and quit jobs and treatments throughout my life if they no longer worked or felt aligned for me. I have jumped into the void…and The Universe has caught me each time. It was through the gift of PTS that I finally started to support myself and allow myself to be supported.

Realigning Exercise: Realigning Needs

Not many of us grow up with the experience of being able to openly express our needs. In many cases, we may not even recognise or know what our real needs are, and we may confuse *wants* with *needs*.

Needs include safety, security, closeness, honesty, love, autonomy, fun, understanding, respect, support, care, integrity, empathy, trust, and to be heard or seen.

- What is the issue (health or otherwise) in your awareness that needs addressing?
- When you think of this issue, where do you feel it in your body?

- Where you feel it, ask your body, "What is the need that I hope to have met?"
  (Refer to the needs listed above if you need a hint.)

There may be multiple needs, so if you feel you have not gotten to the core, keep going until you feel you have. (Feel it land as an *a-ha* or shift of energy.)

Next, ask yourself,

- What lies have I been telling myself in order for it to be okay or less painful not to have this need met?
  It may be along the lines of "I was not good enough/ worthy/deserving of having my needs met" or "I am not loved/lovable/loving."
- What do I need to understand in order to forgive myself for believing or living this lie?
- What do I need to understand in order to forgive others for seeing me and treating me in alignment with this lie?
- Am I willing to have my needs met in a loving way with others and myself?
- What is a truly healthy way I could have this need met?
- Am I willing to receive this and live in the here and now?
- What words of encouragement am I looking for or need?
- What prayer will assist in transforming this?

Speak those words or that prayer and allow yourself to realign with this new truth.

Connect with Rest

In the wisdom of sacred scriptures, the seventh day is assigned as a day of rest. In order to be our joyous selves, we need rest. Let's take back our sacred day of rest!

Rest helps us restore, heal, integrate, and align ourselves.

The message we've been told for years is work hard, do more or miss out, and soldier on (and ignore cold and flu, which is really our body asking for a time-out and rest).

We are shamed as lazy, guilted for taking time off or out, and made to feel no matter how much we do, it is never enough and there is always more we could do or could have done. We are obsessed by *doing* and neglecting *being* human.

Even though we have all these amazing devices to do our work for us and make our lives easier and free up our time, so many speak of being tired, exhausted, fatigued, burned out, stressed, overwhelmed, and wired without enough time to do all the things we need to do. We are hypnotised and hijacked by the very devices that free up our time. We sacrifice rest time to stay up all night to binge shows and series. We are too busy working or being entertained to even recognise the need to slow down or rest, until we are forced to rest by getting sick or injured or we become too tired to function.

For something that comes naturally, rest and sleep is something we have made into a lot of work. Why has it become (another) something we need to work hard at? Treating rest like this creates the opposite effect to what we are seeking.

Our circadian rhythm or body clock gets out of whack by having late nights (or maybe more accurately, early-morning nights) and insufficient rest over extended lengths of time. Cortisol and adrenaline levels are naturally highest in the morning, as they help us to get up and get going. When we consistently use and deplete cortisol and adrenaline reserves by trying to stay awake at night (and get our second wind) we create a state of adrenaline reversal or exhaustion (as it is used up at night rather than restored), making it hard, or near impossible, not just to get to sleep, but also to wake up, get up, and get moving.

Without this natural morning pep, we resort to caffeine and stimulants to energise and wake up. At night we might do the opposite, using alcohol and/or sedating and calming substances to help sleep (although not creating restorative sleep). Note: some people are actually night owls getting optimal sleep in the hours opposite to most (we are not all the same)—know yourself and your body and what it needs.

Today we have apps to track and measure sleep, which might help if we actually addressed the issues those apps display; however, I believe they do more to increase anxiety, so we do not truly rest. Apps suggest we should always sleep in a certain way and so if we don't measure up, we then believe we are doing something wrong or that there is something wrong with us. What sleep apps may not consider is the effect of the lunar cycle on sleep and that we may in fact sleep in cycles. They do not consider the many different ways in which we sleep, and the different things different people need in order to sleep. We can have all the right measurements and stats on the sleep app yet still not wake rested, energised, and ready to go.

Like the smart phone batteries these apps run on, we are not all the same. Cadmium batteries need to be run down to empty to recharge fully and Lithium batteries last longer if kept topped up yet not fully charged or they might combust. Similarly, some people sleep better if they physically "run off" excess energy before going to bed to wake up fully recharged. Others need to lie down before feeling tired in order to sleep. Some sleep better alone.

Sleep research even disagrees on optimal hours of sleep with the standard eight hours under debate. There are disagreements to optimal hours and whether we need to sleep continually or in shifts. Research shows there is not just one formula or way. What was valuable for me, was discovering research that showed how we sleep in one and a half hour blocks and wake up between them (although may be unaware of it). This was a game changer for me as it allowed me to stop being anxious and thinking there was something wrong because I kept waking up every few hours. Knowing this allowed me to simply roll over and go back to sleep rather than make myself wrong or stressed that I was not getting enough sleep.

Sleep requirements vary for individuals (no surprise there) as do age, health, physical exertion, planetary, lunar, and body cycles (e.g., menstrual). How aligned we are in life also impacts how we get to sleep and whether we stay asleep.

There are some things I believe can help (as I have experienced them): sleeping in absolute darkness (helps increase melatonin); using warm light (yellow) and not cool light (white or blue is stimulating or equivalent to daylight); ceasing to use computer or devices with bright or stimulating light a few hours before sleeping; resetting my circadian rhythm by watching sunrise and sunset. These have all helped improve sleep quality and the ability to fall asleep. Although I will add, I do not always do them and even this seems to happen in cycles. One thing is for sure: stressing or punishing yourself for not doing it all does not help.

Maybe we could sleep better if we measured how we feel when we wake up and how well we sustain energy, rather than measuring sleep in numbers and stats and feeling like we are not measuring up.

Do we really need additional work, numbers, stats, and analyses to sleep better? Or do we need to remember that our bodies know how to sleep in the way that is best for us, and that we just need to listen to our bodies better, rather than an app?

Have we become so busy and wired that we have forgotten who we truly are and what is truly important? Are we too busy making a living that we've forgotten to make a life worth living?

The simplest and most natural truth of self-**RESpecT** is rest!

Realigning Exercise:
RestFULLY

———————〜————————

Rest day does not have to be a Sunday. Any day ending in *day* will do, sunny or not. Take back a day to restore yourself. Give yourself *full permission* to do nothing, or to do something that fills your cup, brings you joy, realigns your energy or yourself.

We are not meant to be always on; switch off sometimes.

- Do you ever allow yourself even a single minute to fully rest?
- Can you receive rest?
- Can you just sit or lie and allow your mind to wander, or wonder, without actually directing, attaching meaning, or thinking about it—simply letting it be—being with it, without directing or judging?

- Would it be possible to give yourself *FULL and absolute permission* to do nothing... not even meditate?

So often when we think we are resting, we are in fact thinking (and often a lot)—thinking about what we need to do or have not done or about what to have for dinner or how we need to paint over that crack in the wall.

Do you think you are resting when you are in fact just distracting yourself with technology, games, or various types of entertainment?

When was the last time you just sat fully absorbed?

I find it easiest to achieve this by being fully absorbed in nature—watching a sunset, watching and listening to my horse eat, sitting with nothing to do, think, worry, or care about. Just being with and in nature, even if just a potted plant, a daisy in pavement crack, or a tree in a park.

These moments can be incredibly restorative. It does not have to be for long. A few stolen moments to breathe, reset, and realign yourself and your day can be profoundly restorative.

Be kind and compassionate with yourself, knowing that there is no right or wrong answer, just information, and feel into the following questions:

> *Could you make just thirty seconds (yes, seconds) in your day to fully rest?*

> *Are you willing to take thirty seconds in your day to fully rest, or simply just breathe?*

Remember it is all just information, so no judging. How easy did you find it to say yes?

- Did you come up with any reasons or excuses why you are unable to make 30 seconds in your day?
- Was your response full hearted or convinced? Or wavering and uncertain?

- If unwilling, can you be lovingly curious as to why? What are you protecting yourself from?
- How do you feel about your unwillingness? Where do you feel it in your body? Is there a message in that for you?
- If you could do thirty seconds easily, would you be able to extend that time? A minute? Ten minutes? Fifteen minutes? Half an hour? An hour? At what time do objections start arising?

Losing Your Mind

A common fear these days is regarding mental health—that we may be losing our grip or losing our mind.

We have been educated to predominately think with the reasonable, analytical, scientific, systemic, process-driven, mathematical, factual, or logical mind that builds on what it learns and the knowledge we can learn. Our education system is heavily focused on developing the left hemisphere of the brain; however, it is not even half the brain, let alone half the story.

The creative, illogical, imaginative, intuitive, feeling, and artistic (right hemisphere) functions of the brain have been considered less valuable or important (or maybe more truthfully, less controllable and more difficult to measure and grade). We are starting to see school systems fail as they are less able to cater to increasing numbers of children born with highly developed right brains. The logical system counters this anomaly by labelling it as a problem with the child, rather than a problem with the system. Children are diagnosed with various disorders or disabilities (when it is far from it); however, it does leave many struggling to fit in a system that neither caters to nor appreciates their brilliantly imaginative and illogically creative minds and abilities.

The illogical, imaginative, creative right mind can feel uncomfortable or unsafe when we have learned to rely on predictable, safe logic. Things are changing, as all things do, and the time of the left (masculine) mind being dominant is phasing out, as the right (feminine) mind is phasing in to realign balance. We are not losing our minds; we are *loosening* our minds from limited thinking to gain fuller access.

Many being diagnosed with mental illness see the world in ways the logical mind does not understand and the "trying to make sense of it" can drive them crazy. Many are seen as crazy, as society does not yet have the knowledge to understand, accept, or explain it logically. We need to appreciate the value of the imaginative, creative, and illogical mind, as it is from here we will find new solutions to new and emerging problems and new ways to work with old problems so we can leap out of patterns instead of repeating them.

The logical (left) is great at identifying patterns and creating systems to generate some surety or security in the future. The logical mind tells us day follows night, there are four seasons, spring follows winter, and the moon has a twenty-eight-day cycle. The logical mind uses processes to improve efficiency and effectiveness. Science is logical. Patterns can be measured, tested, and proven.

Have we become too mesmerised, trusting, and entangled by the logical mind? In favouring logic and reason, we are becoming less creative, intuitive, or less able to find a solution to day-to-day problems. Yet, today we cannot learn less from the patterns or past as we are entering rapidly changing uncharted territory.

When we use the abstract, creative (right) mind, we are more commonly told we are living in la-la-land and that our ideas are "mad" or "crazy," or that we are out of our minds, or losing it. Today's society does not fully appreciate or value the creative, sensing, imaginative, and knowing mind. It is considered unreasonable and illogical because the truth is, *it is!* Yet, this does not make it of any less value than the logical mind; in fact, today we need it to find new solutions to new problems, such as *how do we navigate artificial intelligence (AI)?*

Illogical knows the unknown. It senses what cannot be measured and sees what cannot be seen. Just because you cannot reason, measure, or see it does not mean it is not real.

Science is a logical process, relying on facts and measurements to prove a theory. We place a lot of faith in science; however, is it correct to negate something simply because it cannot be measured or proven (... yet)? Science once denied the existence of air until it could be measured. Science has been telling us for some time that 98 percent of our DNA is "junk"... apparently, we are walking, talking, human trash cans.

Perhaps our faith in traditional systems of science and religion, that tell us to trust, believe, and have faith in what they are saying (rather than what we are getting) is misplaced. Does *everything* need to be proven before we believe it? Can we not just trust what is correct for *us*? Can we truly find our way via systems that are outdated, cannot keep up, and seem to have lost their way?

More abstract sciences like quantum physics in many ways questions the effectiveness of the scientific system and process itself. Specifically, that an observer can influence results, proving that the experimenter creates or makes the result they are proving. Plus, with the way the RAS brain works (as discussed earlier), a scientist is more likely to see what they are looking for, and not see what is actually occurring. Science is disproving its own effectiveness every day, yet we remain blind to it.

Logic is valuable, as it helps make the abstract or unknown known, understandable, and sharable. Quantum physics bridges the gap, or is the middle path, between the logical and the abstract, between science and spirituality. In many ways, it proves the validity of spirituality as it investigates the very existence of The Universe and the energy that unites it (and us) all.

Realigning Exercise:
Mental Fitness

Have you noticed with the apps and brain training techniques to sharpen our minds, they are actually training us to think less, or to think without thinking?

They are training us to "think" more instinctively or intuitively (not working it out logically and sequentially), which is in contradiction to what is being taught at school, where even though children can have the correct answer, they cannot receive full marks unless they can show the workings (which many cannot do because it all happens so quickly in their heads they cannot slow it down enough to "catch" it). Many children are thought to be or are told they are stupid, when they are in fact far from it and quite the opposite, finding the way of education too slow and futile as they are way ahead of it.

You would not go to the gym and only work one side of your body unless there was a physical reason to do so. Can you see the nonsense of "the old school ways" only really training and working one side of our brain?

Fortunately, it is never too late to work on your brain fitness, as the brain is incredibly malleable and adaptive (neuroplastic). It does not have to be costly in time or money, nor do you need fancy apps. Start your brain fitness now by creating or inventing ways to engage both sides of your brain in different ways.

To get you started:

- Do with your left, what you can do with your right (or vice versa). It is not just about left and right handedness (e.g., brushing teeth); it is also about:
  - leading or stepping out with the non-dominant foot;

- changing the direction you automatically or usually go (supermarkets are actually designed around our natural bias);
- alternating a route or a circuit (if you walk a regular circuit, walk or run in the opposite direction from what you usually do).
- What can you do better with your non-dominant hand? (I can snap the fingers on my left hand, yet not my right, which is ironic seeing though it is my dominant one.)

If at first you do not succeed, keep giving it a go; you will amaze yourself one day. I once worked as a roulette dealer or croupier at a casino, and we had to learn to deal, spin, cut, pick up, and push chips with both hands (due to left- and right-handed tables). Initially it was awkward, slow, and clumsy; yet after a month, the speed, precision, and flair were far superior with my left than my right.

Fitness of mind is also about developing and enhancing our intuitive senses. So be creative about the many ways in which you might be able to tune in, strengthen, and develop your sense of vision, smell, taste, feel, and hearing.

How could you feel into the energy or frequencies of these more and rely less on physical tangible form. For example:

- Be more attuned to when your plants need or are asking for water.
- Know when something is ready or cooked by smell, rather than just time and sight.
- See if you know who is calling before you look at your phone.
- Intuit the best way to drive home today (not always taking the same route).
- Get a feel for right (or divine) timing.

- Use your senses in different and imaginative ways, like "tasting" or "smelling" the right colour to wear today (I don't mean physically tasting or smelling but simply asking those senses to inform you, such as if you thought of red, you may have the sensation of heat or taste or smell red; whatever that means to you). If it tastes or smells good, good. If it doesn't, then find another colour.

I used to say: "We need to lose our minds and come to our senses." Now I say: "We need to loosen our minds and widen our senses."

How would you say it?

Truth

Do you know what truth is? Do you know how to tell what is true and what is not?

We are living in a world where it is becoming increasingly difficult to know what is true and what is not, as we are fed so many lies and the truth is often masked, attacked, or labelled as a conspiracy or not scientific. Many things we thought were true are increasingly being revealed to be not true, partially true, or straight out lies.

Mainstream media does more than tell news, it casts spells and lies and reveals partial truths. News will saturate us through telling us the same thing repeatedly; yet just because it is told a thousand times, does not mean it is true. We are more likely to think it is if we do not actively question it. Is it safe? Effective? If you find yourself vehemently defending a so-called truth, chances are it is not true (and you feel or know it), but you are entangled in it, or the ego is so invested in a lie it wants to be true it is willing to fight for it. Truth does not need defending—it just is. Truth is felt, not thought. Sometimes the truth is uncomfortable, and it is actually our comfort that we are defending, rather than truth.

Some of the more everyday truths or lies we face are whether this text, email, or link is genuine or spam, phishing or malware. Without knowing how or why, one way you can detect whether it is or not, is by being aware of how it feels. Your intuition and instincts will tell you what is truth and what is not. Your mind only *thinks* it knows. Learn to listen to your body, the twinge in your gut, the tight squeeze in the heart, the jangled senses.

A truth to become more familiar and comfortable with is—truth is paradox. Everything is true and nothing is. You may discover at the spiritual or universal level that truth is somewhat paradoxical, everything means nothing and nothing means everything, opposites are equally true, and miracles can bend truths.

Paradox is something difficult for the logical this-or-that left brain to fathom. The abstract right brain is more equipped for greater truths, such as that *this* can be *both* this *and* that, such as an atom can be a particle *and* a wave. Something incomprehensible in the beginning can become accepted as truth as the logical mind catches up and comprehends or at least accepts.

There is great joy in knowing and being in your truth. The key is in knowing there is no single or absolute truth but many levels of truth. There is personal, collective, soul, and universal truth. What may be true at one level may not be true on another. For example, your personal truth may be that nuts are poisonous (if allergic); however, the collective truth says nuts are food. At the soul level, nuts are considered seeds of life, not food; and at the universal level, there is no nut, as it is all that is.

If your personal truth is the only truth you believe, you have limited understanding. Personal truth is based on your experience and what you know or believe to be true. What is true for you, may not be true for another; however, neither person's truth is less true. You are best not to follow another's truth, especially if you are allergic to nuts.

Learn to align with the truth and level of truth that feels right for you without negating the truth of another. It can be healthy to be righteous and stand in your truth, yet unhealthy to stand in self-righteous indignation.

Do not be fooled into believing truth can be found via the mind. The mind is dualistic, it flip-flops, and it can argue for or against anything as is so well demonstrated in the art of debate. Every subject has multiple viewpoints that are true, including opposite and opposing ones which can be argued in the affirmative or negative.

Truth is not opinion.

Truth is not emotional.

Truth does not need to be defended.

Feel the truth in your heart and gut. Connect and reconnect through your intuition. The truth can be hard to handle, as it is not absolute (except maybe at the universal level) and is often starkly confronting. Truth has a clarity which changes with experience and understanding. Hold truth lightly, not tightly, rigidly, or inflexibly. Allow it to expand and grow with you. Your truth today, may not be your truth tomorrow and can be very different again next week, month, or year as your experiences change your perceptions and truth builds upon truth.

It is said that truth can set you free. Certainly, when you connect with the truth that feels aligned with you, it can help you align with the truth that *is* you and the joy that generates.

Realigning Exercise:
Connecting to Your Truth

Do not make everything you read your truth (including everything in this book!). Use your senses and discernment as to whether something feels true to you or not.

To learn to connect with your truth, start asking and feeling into the question:

"Does this feel true for me?"

Today it can be difficult to determine what is true and what is a lie, or what is real and what is not. We need to ask "truth or lie?" of nearly everything that pops up in our face, feed, thread, notification, email, text, or messages and whether it is genuine or not.

To help navigate the invasion of spam and scams, it helps to become aware of your spontaneous body sensations, reactions, and responses on initial encounter as everything comes with an energetic imprint and you feel it whether you are conscious of it or not.

Have you ever avoided opening an email or message for reasons unknown and upon reading, found angry, attacking, shocking, bad, distressing, or unwanted content? Have you ever opened or read the first line of an email and instantly felt yourself recoiling, contracting, or defending? Or felt uneasy, queasy, uncomfortable, or a sense of feeling attacked or violated even before reading another word? You are reading the energy imprint, and it is this energy imprint that can also guide you to what is genuine or true and what is not.

You tune into and know intuitively much more than you think you do, as you are always receiving information or data from everything in your environment. To navigate this world of information and misinformation, you need to be more highly attuned to your senses and knowing.

Knowledge is helpful in recalling what you have learned; however, it only knows what it knows. *Knowing* and *knowledge* are not the same. *Knowledge* is conscious, cognitive, and learned or thought. *Knowing* is unconscious, intuitive, and revealed or felt as clarity. You need finer attunement by reading each incidence as things can look the same yet feel very different.

Take special note of how or what you *feel or sense energetically* when you see, open, read, or encounter something (have your bullsh!t detector turned on).

If fear or intense reaction is activated, take time to check in and gain clarity. Only take action when you have clarity and feel emotionally neutral or at least calmer and settled. Spam and scam correspondence often has a shock value asking for immediate action, and so can some genuine ones. Do your research first, such as checking your bank account to see if you actually did pay the bill you just received a late notice for.

You will need to find out for yourself what *truth* and *genuine* feel like to you and build, train, and hone your truth-finding fitness. Generally, truth feels unemotional, unreactive, and clear, so work from there and find how it feels for you.

Insightful Acceptance

A two-year-old (needing help to manage their overwhelm from all the information they are sensing in their environment and not being able to find their centre to calm or emotionally regulate themselves) tries to get their mother's attention. The child is told to be quiet or is ignored, as mum (who needs uninterrupted time to remember what she needs to get) continues shopping. The two-year-old nags for lollies (as it might give them the dopamine hit they need to distract them from escalating emotions and overwhelm with the added stress of being admonished or ignored). Mum snaps "No!" (feeling overwhelmed and frustrated as her need to be uninterrupted is ignored and she is unable to get the clarity of mind she needs to remember what she needs to get for a two-year-old).

Do you see the escalation of needs as each goes unacknowledged?

One thing we all crave is to be noticed, acknowledged, and accepted as we are. As children, our whole strategy is based on being noticed by others so they can take care of us. Being accepted for who and how we are becomes a secondary priority if we cannot have both at the same time. It does not cease just because we grow up into adults. We still crave to be noticed and even more so to be accepted for who we are. Yet, in so many ways, we do not accept *ourselves* for who or how we are.

Those things that are not acknowledged or accepted do not necessarily go away. Emotions are like messengers that want to communicate something to us (like the two-year-old); however, if we ignore, deny, or disregard this message, it gets stored and filed away. We are then sent reminders (in the form of pain) as if to say "you need to look over here because there is a message for you." And, therefore, pain, wounds, illness, disease, addictions, and trauma, at their core, are simply what we have not noticed, acknowledged, or accepted about ourselves.

In a way there is little difference between the emotion and the two-year-old. A lot of wounds are laid down during the first six years of our lives when we are less able to express what we are needing or wanting and are also unable to regulate the emotions from not having those needs met.

Getting back to *everything is energy and the emotional two-year-old:* when emotions are unnoticed or ignored, things amp up and escalate in order to be acknowledged over the other noise and distractions. The body escalates its signalling as its needs are ignored or dismissed. It asks for rest or time-out, expressing this through cold or flu symptoms.

Instead of taking rest, you soldier on ignoring or denying the body's request for time-out. The cold may escalate all the way to pneumonia and guess who ends up sick in bed, or hospital, and the body says "ahhh—rest at last!"

Unfortunately, many still fail to acknowledge the needs of the body and so who knows what will come next?

Insightful acceptance is a profound form of radical spiritual parenting, which means re-parenting the wounded or ignored parts of ourselves by lovingly noticing what is there behind the pain, then acknowledging the message as intelligent and important and accepting it as it is, without criticism or judgement.

It helps to remember that all energy is neutral and that the source of all energy is originally love, and all is happening *for* you (not *to* you). Allow yourself to discover the loving messages and gifts your wounds, sicknesses, addictions, and traumas; as difficult as it might be, see them all as loving messengers helping you to gain greater acceptance of who and what you are.

Each is a loving messenger showing you the way and helping you align with what is true, genuine, and authentic for you.

Realigning Exercise: The Healing Formula

You may have noticed this formula applied through other exercises in this book already. This simple yet very effective formula (based on the foundational hexagram of the Chinese I Ching) can be applied to almost any situation, event, illness, wound, ailment, pain, or trauma and help you move through energies promoting and creating healing and transformation.

Six simple and effective steps to transform the energy:

1. Notice.
2. Acknowledge.
3. Accept
    … willingness to change.
4. Forgive.
5. Imagine.
6. Embody wisdom.

Alternatively, with loving curiosity, you may follow this line of inquiry:

1. What do I need to be aware of?
2. What do I feel? Where do I feel it?

3. Can I accept what has happened? Is it okay for me to feel how I feel? (If not, why not?)

   Then ... How would I *like* to feel instead? Am I willing to?

4. Who or what do I need to forgive? Can I forgive myself?

5. Can I imagine how I would *like* to feel, i.e., joyous, free, and loving?

6. Can I allow my body to feel the wisdom of this new way of being?

Complete Responsibility

In nature and the animal kingdom, there are no victims, and there is no blame or guilt.

I heard somewhere that prey gives their predator "permission," which I found difficult to fathom until I saw it on a big cat documentary. A lion was stalking a herd of gazelles, and the camera was following it. The lion and cameras locked on one. The gazelle shivered. The lion crept forward. The gazelle stomped its foot. The lion leaped. The gazelle took flight. The lion chased. It was subtle but the shiver and sequence of events seemed to support the idea. Acknowledgment of permission or challenge? Catch me if you can.

It got me thinking about bullying at school and my experience both of being bullied and being the bully. Was I unconsciously giving permission by sending out a shiver? Was I seeing it from the other? Is this why some people are targets and others who equally could be are not? What energy exchange is happening unconsciously in all of this?

I wonder what changed in the years I was bullied, and the years I was not, as bullying was still happening around me. When I feel into it, I see the young me, with high sensitivity and low self-worth feeling insecure, wrong, and weakened in my differences. Maybe I toughened up. Maybe I got braver. Maybe I cared less or got better at not being seen. I did also get better at handling the bullying, reacting less, and pretending I was unbothered by it, which gave them less fuel. It may also have been the improving self-esteem (or did my self-esteem improve when I reacted less?).

Being bullied may be seen as an opportunity to work on self-worth and esteem. Because all is energy and energy exchange, and in order to *be* a bully, the bully needs a victim. If the bullied is no longer a victim, there is no bully. The victim has a lot of unrealised potential power here. There is great gain in improving self-esteem and healing traumas even if it does not stop the bullying (although from experience I believe it does).

Even in my late forties, my sibling still teased me about a particular photograph, and I still reacted to their teasing. I no longer wanted to be bothered by it, so I took the photo and made it my phone's wallpaper so I would see it all the time. It was like the photo changed over time. The weird little girl leaning in, became endearing and even cute in her wrinkled bathers, photo bombing before it was a thing. I used the photo for my fiftieth birthday invitation and sent it to all my family. I receive no comments about that or any other photo since.

It is strange how we can torture ourselves over things that when really looked at, are not that big a deal or even what we thought they were. Thanks to my "mean" siblings, I got to spend time with and learn to love and accept the little girl who wanted to stand alone yet also be included. I got to reembrace an abandoned part of self.

Realigning Exercise:
Responsibility and Understanding

We will start with the basics: everything is energy. Energy is not personal, yet it is felt very intimately.

If you are having difficulty in a relationship, it may help to ask: What energy is playing out between us? This is not a game of blame or shame. Keep to straightforward, unemotional, impersonal facts. No embellishments, story, or words like *because*.

"When I heard X say <quote accurately>, I felt <name feeling; e.g., hurt>."

Notice it is *not* "They made me feel hurt when they said _____" or "Because they said _____, it hurt me." Or "When they said that, it meant _____." No blame. Just facts.

The aim of this exercise is to take full responsibility for:

- what you heard,
- how you heard it,
- what YOU made that to mean to YOU, and,
- how you reacted or responded to it.

This lived example below has been written in this factual non-emotional way with a lot of *I*. It also demonstrates how what we *think* we are saying can be interpreted and made to mean something different from our intention. As we each hear through our own filters, it helps to clarify how another is interpreting it, instead of assuming we are thinking the same way.

My partner seemed upset after I asked him to ask his son to pick up his shoes from the middle of the doorway, after he had not responded to my request.

I do not recall his reply; however, it looked like he seemed upset and angry.

I thought that what I had said was fair and wanted to clarify the situation.

I asked, "May I ask, what did you hear me say and what did you think I meant by it?"

He replied, "That you think I am a bad father."

I assured him this was not what I meant nor thought. I just wanted the shoes out of the doorway, and my direct request had not been attended to.

I ensured that I assured him of his parenting, and I no longer sensed he was upset when I made requests regarding his sons.

When the energy is changed, there is no longer the same energy to attract the opposite. If you do not react in the same way, they no longer get the energy they are seeking, and it's a new dance!

Patience

At first look, patience may not seem like a life-changing trait or even a trait of great importance; however, the difference patience has made in my life and relationships is phenomenal.

I am extremely grateful to have been shown and to have learned patience. My guide and teacher in patience was a horse who taught me what I do not believe I could have learned from a human (as I would have been too impatient to be taught). Learning patience has allowed me to deepen my relationships, not just with animals, but with people and situations.

An impatient mind can receive as much as a closed fist. In order to truly be in the flow of life and allow life's events to unfold, we must learn patience. If you wish to manifest what you truly want, you need to wait. You can wait patiently or impatiently. It's your choice. However, waiting patiently brings greater rewards. *Ah, the joys of waiting.*

We are actually *designed* to wait. We are human *be*-ings not human *do*-ings, remember? While we are waiting, we can do other things, such as play, love, rest, imagine, create, and anything else that raises our vibration, so that we are in such a state we attract what will bring us happiness and allow our joy to emerge. If you can joyously wait, more power to you.

Pushing. Forcing. Striving. Controlling. Manipulating. Scheming. Planning. We have been taught to be active and do, do, *do*. And although it is true—we do need to take action—we are best to do so only *when the timing is right*.

In the meantime, it is often a case of wait patiently and do our best not to tug at the growing shoots and uproot the project or pull it out too early. Patience is something that nature has in spades. Everything in nature has its time and timing which cannot be hastened; only humans are in a hurry to get somewhere just to arrive dissatisfied as they have missed the whole trip.

Realigning Exercise: Divine Timing

We can wait patiently or impatiently and anything that can help us wait more patiently is useful. A technique many clients and friends have been glad I shared is the practice of being there at the best time or "divine time."

I do not like being too early or too late for appointments and events; however, despite my best efforts to be on time, things do not always go to plan or schedule.

The practice of divine timing is about letting go of the concept of *early* or *late* and instead acting in divine time with the intention being to arrive in the time that is mutually favourable (or divinely orchestrated) for all parties.

Here are a few examples of how it has worked for me.

While stuck in traffic on my way to a class, I was slowly working my way up to a set of traffic lights. Having watched about three sets of change, I realised at this rate I was going to be late, and it looked like I was going to have to sit out another set as I was about thirty cars back. I said to The Universe something like "If I'm meant to go to this class, can I please get there on time?" As the traffic lights changed to green, all the cars in front changed lanes and I was left sitting in a clear lane. I cruised through that set and every other set of lights like I was the only person on the road. I arrived in perfect (or divine) time.

Another day on my way to an appointment for which I had left early and thought I had plenty of time, I got stuck in traffic because of an earlier accident. Traffic was not moving or moving very slowly. There was nowhere to exit the freeway and I started to stress about being late. So, I activated divine timing by asking to arrive in divine timing. As there was nothing else I could do, I turned on the radio and decided to enjoy the rest of the drive. Traffic worked past the block and then it was clear sailing and I arrived twenty minutes late from my appointed time. As I was standing at reception, my naturopath walked in and said, "Come straight through."

I apologised for being late and he replied, "So glad you were. I needed lunch and a break and if you were on time, I would not have taken it." Divine timing at work!

Sometimes I need just a bit more time before someone arrives and so I ask for it. There are numerous times I have asked and then got a text message saying they were running a few minutes late. I believe we are often late, not because we are tardy, but because we are meant to be or because someone is asking us to be.

I invite you to give it a go. Divine timing is as simple as asking and going with the flow, being patient, and responding as needed which is easier when you don't have to listen to the ticking clock.

It works on faith, trust, and patience and the intention and knowing that all is working in divine and perfect timing.

How could you use divine timing in your life?

Re-parent Yourself (Self-parent)

Regardless of the parenting we experienced as a child, we always have the opportunity to re-parent ourselves in a different, preferred, or more functional way.

It is easy to keep blaming our parents and others for something that hurt us deeply. Some offences we take hold of, take to heart, and make our truth (whether we actually believe it or not). We continue to blame them, failing to recognise it is now ourselves, *not them* repeating and strengthening our beliefs and behaviours. We may think it untrue, yet keep it alive by telling ourselves we are hopeless, useless, bad, or _____ .

Someone may have said a cruel, heartless, or abusive thing, but please recognise that if they are not in your home, proximity, or earshot right now, it is not *them* giving it the power. If you are the only one in the room, it is *you* being cruel, heartless, or even abusive towards yourself.

Yes, when someone originally said it, it hurt and impacted you, so be loving, tender, and gentle with yourself. Remember: It is not your fault. We are programmed for negativity as a survival mechanism, and we can become enmeshed or entangled with deep wounding or trauma. When we repeat these things, we regress to the age of our childhood abuse, so we do not have the knowledge or resources of our now-adult self.

Awareness is key. Stop the self-abuse by re-parenting yourself and telling yourself what you need.

Realigning Exercise:
Inner Critic

Now that you are aware, when you hear these critical voices start up, question them:

- Is it even true?

- Am I truly <hopeless/useless/etc.>__?

- When was I not <hopeless/useless/etc.>__?

- Is there a payoff I get from repeating this to myself? (E.g., not taking responsibility, having permission to <fail/not stand up for yourself/stand out/be seen>)

- Yes, it was painful to hear <what was said> and it may or may not be true, but why do I keep repeating it? Do I even believe it? Is it valid or true?

Time to perform random acts of self-love and kindness. Say loving and nice things about yourself in contradiction or opposition to what you have been saying. Acknowledge it was and still is painful. No need to keep saying it; instead, say something different. Change the record.

Yes, you may need to find a new language. Yes, you may need to find new things to say to yourself. Yes, it may feel incredibly clunky. Yes, you will revert to old ways and habits. Yes, it will take time. And yes, it will be so worth the initial discomfort!

Find a new loving language. Whether you had "good" parents or not, recruit your internal parents. Choose the words of encourage-ment and speak to yourself in ways you would like to be parented.

We are never too old to have great inner parents. Create the internal dialogue of the nurturing, loving, inclusive, kind, encouraging mother. Create the practical internal dialogue, loving limits, and boundaries of the father. The loving voice that says, "Time for bed. You know you will feel much better in the morning if you go to bed now instead of staying up all night bingeing another series that you can also watch tomorrow."

I will warn you there are some side effects to better self-parenting. One is that you may start feeling better about yourself. You may also become a better parent to your children or find you are more loving and accepting towards your parents.

Relationships can help us access our greatest joy, so work on your relationship with yourself and the voices you are in a relationship with. It is never too late, nor too soon, to create joyous, loving relationships. Start with the relationships you live with all the time—those in your head and heart.

Willingness

How many times have you said you intend to do something, really want to do something, or know you need to do something, yet you don't do it? We may think if we have the desire or the need that we will do it; however, willingness has the final say. Without willingness we do not have the will and thus it will be unlikely to happen.

Without 100 percent willingness to follow through with the action it takes to be what we want to be, we may not see it through to the end. We may start enthusiastically and drop off or give up before the finish line. Without willingness there is no resolve or will to work through the tough spots, discomforts, or obstacles to see it through.

I see willingness as the more passive (feminine) energy of will-power which creates the path when we are aligned with our desires and needs. I see will as the more active (masculine) energy or power activated and actioned to keep realigning to the path we have chosen.

You can have the will and say you want to get better and do the work to get better, and you can be very busy doing all the "right" things; however, if any part within is unaligned or lacks willingness to get better, you may sabotage or lack the grit to see it through to the end to gain the results you are wanting or needing.

It's important to remember lack of willingness is usually a result of not feeling safe in some way. Even though it is what they really want to do, someone may be unwilling to try working for themselves as an energetic healer or alternative therapist, not because they don't think they are capable, but because it says to the world "this is what I believe." Although it may seem irrelevant today, there has been a long, dark history of persecution for those beliefs and practices in our collective consciousness that still smoulders, causing those who are sensitively attuned to feel unsafe.

Realigning Exercise: How Willing Am I?

If you are ever facing something important in your life, ask yourself tender and compassionate questions like:

Do I absolutely want to do or be this (e.g., to get well or be healthy and joyous)?

Am I 100 percent willing to do what is required (e.g., to get well or be healthy and joyous)?

Tune in and listen to your response (what you say, how you say it, and how you feel).

If it is not a definitive yes, treat it as a no and worthy of further gentle enquiry.

Please do not judge yourself or make yourself wrong regarding any lack of willingness. You may describe what is revealed as surprising or curious, rather than wrong or crazy.

Remember it is most likely because of something you fear—it takes courage to go against the status quo, as we have been so heavily conditioned against our own self-care and being joyous. Our unwillingness may come from our childhood or circumstances where it was not safe to be healthy or joyous.

You can further this self-enquiry by gently checking in with yourself:

- What do I fear? What am I protecting myself from?
- What am I afraid might happen if_____ (e.g., I am healthy or joyously happy)?

Tenderness and empathy! No criticism or judgement. Self-parent and give yourself the loving encouragement you need to hear so that you can move past this—if you are willing or have willingness!

Give yourself unconditional love for whatever is showing up for you right now. This is not a time to push through wilfully. True willingness is a joyous release, not a punishing push.

Right or Happy?

A pivotal question to ask when deciding whether to forge ahead, let something go, or when disagreements come up in relationships, work, or other areas of life, is this:

Do I want to be right, or do I want to be happy?

The ego wants to be right, and the true self and soul wants to be happy and joyous. We have been conditioned to believe we have to fight for justice, happiness, and what is right. This is fraught with danger as what one considers to be just or right, may differ from another's idea. Or we may "win," yet still feel justice has not been carried out or feel robbed of the happiness we are seeking by being right.

Right and wrong are very subjective and not something everyone agrees upon. What is right for one, can be wrong for another. Ensure you also make the distinction that being wrong about something does *not* mean that *you* are wrong.

It is vitally important to question or ask whether a fight is worth having or not.

If the process of fighting the good fight will feel satisfying (not in the smug way) and bring happiness in some way, and if it is the fight, more than the result, that is of vital importance to you, then go for it.

If you are desperate for a specific outcome (yours) and are more determined to prove that you are right and they are wrong, then surrendering and conserving your energy might lead you to greater happiness and satisfaction (as it is your ego talking and the ego is rarely satisfied or happy for very long).

There is a huge difference between fighting for right and fighting to *prove* you are right.

The question of right or happy can help achieve enduring and lasting peace. When you find doubt about your choice creeping in, ask it again—and ask it as many times you need to ensure you maintain alignment with your decision.

Your ego may kick up a storm and try to make you fall into old habits or patterns or trap or entangle you into being right or proving yourself right. Yes, you are allowed to change your mind— if it feels truly aligned to do so (and it is not your ego talking).

Realigning Exercise: When Desires and Happy Clash

Getting what we desire is not a guarantee for happiness. In fact, often it leads to unhappiness or short-lived happiness.

You may know it—when you really desire to meet, date, or have something (or someone) and your desire is so strong it over-powers your senses. And you meet, date, or get that something or someone and it is not all it was cracked up to be and is a disappointment— you are neither happy, nor happy about it.

To gain enduring happiness from a desire, you need to first align with that desire and where it is coming from: Is it a heady, physical, emotional, or soul desire? They all have their place; however, if you are attached and entangled in one specific outcome where nothing else will do—you may be setting yourself up for disappointment.

To align more happily with your desires, it may help to be open to other possibilities or variations, which may even prove to be better than what you wanted or desired. "Ask and it is given." When we ask God or The Universe for what we desire, need, or want, it is given to us, yet not always in the way we imagine or want.

Unpack the whole box, don't just open it, and if what is on top is not what you had in mind, throw it away. Your desire might be at the bottom of the box, and what you unpack before it, might be just what you need to enable you to truly appreciate and create enduring happiness with that which you desire.

More commonly, we do not truly know what we desire and so do not recognise it when it comes our way.

- What do you desire?
- What about it will make you happy?
- Does it have to be a specific way?
- What are the vitally important elements?

For example, if your desire is for a partner and you have distilled down that what would make you happy are four essential things:

1. Intellectual stimulation; where we can learn and teach one another to grow and improve and be better people.
2. Have integrity and emotional compatibility; being of service and support each other and also have a love or passion for something in life.
3. Sexual (not just physical) attraction.
4. Circumstances and timing are compatible (i.e., available, not married, live locally).

And if you had these four things, would it really matter to your happiness if they were tall or short, had blue or brown eyes, blonde, red, or no hair? If you find them sexually, mentally, and emotionally attractive, do you really need any specifics of what they look like? Does the packaging matter when it's what is in the box that matters and it's all there?

Relationship with Self

The *most* important relationship is the relationship you have with yourself. How can we have world peace when we are at war *within* ourselves?

We criticise and say things about ourselves, and in ways we would never speak to another. We blame others for saying terrible things about us or to us yet say worse things to and about ourselves all the time.

Remember: Words are powerful. What you say matters. Your mind operates like Google, taking notice of everything you say or interact with, and then customising what you see and come across (because it is what you want).

If you continue to play on repeat things others have said, it becomes part of you whether you believe it to be true or not. Let it go, heal it, or change it; no longer give it airplay, and your reality will change.

Any time you spend on improving what you say to and about yourself is time well spent as it will also improve your relationship with yourself and others. How you do one thing is how you do all things. Improve one relationship, and it improves *all* relationships. Your relationship with yourself is the only relationship where you have full VIP access and backstage passes.

Before attempting to change others, remember that when you point a finger at another, you point three at yourself. Be the change you want to see. When you change ... *they* may change.

Although we may not think so, in relationships we relate more energetically than personally. This comes back to *everything is energy*. When we change ourselves, we change our energy. This changes the way we relate in relationships; we change the dance. It only takes one to change the steps of a dance, but it takes two to maintain the dance in a relationship.

There are essentially four ways the dance can go when you take the lead:

- Change step – they dance your dance with you.
- Introduce new steps – lead a change to create a new dance.
- Make a backstep – change back to an old familiar dance.
- Fall out of step – leave the dance floor.

Many do not dance in relationships because they fear the other leaving the dance floor. When you take the lead in your life and value your relationship with yourself, you will rejoice in dancing with yourself and/or with a worthy dance partner.

Realigning Exercise:
Dancing with Yourself

Do you save your best encouragement, compliments, and loving words for others and not yourself? If so, why?

What encouraging, loving, or complimentary words could you say to yourself right now?

Write down or say to yourself (in the mirror if you can) something encouraging, loving, or complimentary every day this week.

Do you speak with yourself in the same way you speak with your best friend? If not, why not?

Do you appreciate your own efforts as greatly as you appreciate others? If not, why not?

What do you most appreciate about yourself?

List all the things you find easy to do (especially those that others may not find easy).

Remember the degree of difficulty has nothing to do with the value or strength of the gifts. Things we are most gifted at are usually the things we find easy or have the ease of willingness to make the time and do the work to embody them.

From your list, what are your gifts or genius?

Help Others

A great source of joy comes from feeling deeply connected with others and experiencing the feeling of being truly, honestly, and authentically connected, supported, seen, or witnessed by another.

To feel like you can be free to let it all hang out, be yourself, and be known, understood, heard, and accepted as and for who you are is profoundly healing and liberating.

Few of us get to experience what it is like to be truly supported or allowed to be the way we are. Few of us know someone whom we trust and feel comfortable enough with to be fully vulnerable.

I find it incredibly sad that many never experience the deeply transformative and supportive presence of having another person be present and honour you as you cry or express your feelings. We need to stop shaming crying, feelings, and emotions because they are the most healthy and therapeutic things we have access to in releasing stored energy and relieving our heart and soul.

The greatest gift we can give another is to be present, hold sacred space, allow them to cry freely and openly, and sit in the sh!t with them. And the deepest honour another can give to you is to trust and respect you enough to share their deepest feelings. We should not have to cry alone. To be allowed to unapologetically cry and be messy in the accepting open loving presence of another is a truly rare gift.

Few of us grow up with role models able to show us how to be truly present with another in crisis. More commonly, our experiences with emotions are having another attempt to make us feel better by joking, fixing, solving, placating, or stopping us from feeling.

As emotional support, it can feel excruciatingly uncomfortable to do nothing and just sit and be with another's intense emotions. However, we must not let this stop us from learning how to get (a least a bit more) comfortable with the discomfort of others' feelings, and the discomfort we feel in feeling theirs. We need to acknowledge how we are feeling, instead of suppressing, denying, or hiding.

We have also not been taught how to *truly* listen. We have become a society of talkers who do not know how to communicate. So many are striving to be heard, yet they are not always worth listening to, as they rarely speak from the heart. Many do not make the time to truly listen to another and listen with presence, often paying more attention to the conversation in their own heads than to what the other is saying or sharing.

Many are unable to hear others over their own internal busy chatter judging, comparing, formulating a response, answer, or fix. Feeling the pressure of wanting to share their own experience—the "I know," "OMG, that happened to me too," or "If you think that was bad, what about this?" It can take considerable practice and presence to listen in silence and become comfortable not saying anything unless truly necessary.

Many never have the opportunity to really get to the depth of what they want to share as they keep getting cut off. To be with another in emotional crisis, you need to allow a lot of time and that may mean a lot of silence.

Although many of us have not been taught or raised to be accepting and comfortable with the uncomfortable feelings, it is something that is vital to improve our mental health, well-being, and fitness.

Much of our so-called mental health issues are really emotions that have been mentally overridden, unaccepted, or not allowed. Feeling sad, grief, depressed, or withdrawn occasionally is vital to our health and creativity, yet we keep being told we should not feel this way, that it is bad and there is something wrong with us.

To truly help others and create deeper relationships, we also need to develop the skills within ourselves to be vulnerable enough to share our feelings with others, *and* we need to develop the capacity to be more comfortable with our uncomfortable feelings, so that we can remain present with our vulnerability and the vulnerability of others.

Vulnerability requires openness, honesty, and presence and is best matched with openness, respect, and compassion creating a powerful portal to deep connection and communion between people.

It is incredibly sad (and disempowering) that we have been taught to not cry or that it is shameful or something to hide, as truly *the* greatest healing and loving gift we can be given, and that we can give another, is to not have to cry alone.

A common practice in tribal and healing circles which would be helpful to use more widely and broadly, is the use of a "talking stick" where only the person holding the stick may speak and it is the role of others to listen and hold space for the person talking.

How great would it be if we could all feel comfortable crying with another and have the other able to hold space while remaining emotionally regulated themselves, so we could really be okay with crying and emotional expression.

Realigning Exercise:
How to Be Present with Another in Emotional Crisis

The greatest support and service you can provide another is to simply be present with them. This means to be calm, centred, and grounded within yourself and to simply allow, accept, and acknowledge where they are and how they are feeling right in the moment.

Be with them without attempting to fix them or change how they are feeling. Just give them full permission to cry, express their feelings, or sit in silence without interruption.

An important thing to remember that can help with alleviating the stress of a person thinking they must go into solution or fix-it mode is to know that if they have the problem, they also have the solution to it. They themselves actually have the solution within already, and often in the process of expressing what they are feeling, the solution arises and that which was blocking or stopping them from accessing their own solution and wisdom is liberated.

We are not given anything we cannot handle, and the solution and problem coexist (as equal and opposite energy). People look predominately for connection and catharsis, not solutions.

Once you truly get that there is nothing for you to do but simply be present, it will come as a huge relief to you and your nervous system. Be here—*I can do that*. Be silent—*I can do that.* What a relief that I do not have to find a solution or fix them.

Although all below have their place, it is all about good *timing*. Be on alert for when you might be tempted to pull out one of these to appease your own discomfort or attempt to change or stop them (rather than be truly helpful) by offering things like the following:

- Platitudes: i.e., "You will see, it will be okay"; "There is nothing to worry about"; "Don't worry"; "You will get over it"; "It will all be over soon."
- Advice or solutions: "Just do this"; "Have you thought of or tried X?"; "This worked for X"; "X did this."
- Minimalising: "It's nothing"; "X's was much worse"; "What are you crying about that for?"; "This can't be the worst thing that ever happened."
- Joking: "What does the other one look like?"
- Distraction or changing the subject.
- Hugging or holding when they have not invited or asked for it.

Be silent and present so that you can gauge the situation and achieve better timing. It is generally a good idea to not offer advice unless they ask you. Alternatively, if you feel a strong, calm, energetic invitation, or nudge to share, wait for an opening and ask them first if they would like you to share before doing so.

They might know what to do, but don't know how or have access to do it in their current state. It is more empowering to guide them in finding their own way, rather than telling them (unless they are so overwhelmed and need the first step—one step may be all they can hear or take on at this stage). Your job is simply to *be* there; you do not have to say or do anything (in most cases, it's best not to).

Allow them to direct you in whether it is appropriate and if they feel comfortable with you holding or comforting them. Physical touch is not always comfortable or comforting. If you feel that holding their hand, hugging, or placing a hand on their back or shoulder might help—**ASK first**, as physical contact can disrupt the flow or trigger other intense feelings for some. Even if you know them well and they usually prefer physical support, still ask, or wait for them to ask or give you a cue.

If you are in the support or witnessing role and intense feelings or discomfort come up for you, do your best to acknowledge them for yourself and hold space for yourself while also being present and holding space for the other. If things get too intense you may be better to excuse yourself, maybe telling them that you will come back and check in with them later.

And a last note. There is a huge difference between them dumping and sharing. Dumping comes from the head (not the heart) and includes blaming (world or others) for what is happening to them, without taking personal responsibility. It is more of a rant and very one-sided and can feel jagged, heavy, and draining for the observer. You may also find yourself getting angry, frustrated, or bitter. If you do feel dumped on, extract yourself gracefully from this situation or person, as dumping rarely changes or helps anyone, as it is not transformed through being felt.

Sharing is expressing from the heart while taking some form of responsibility for feelings and actions. Anger, frustration, and other intense emotions may still be present; however, they are not as sharply pointed or as heavy as when they are dumped. When someone is sharing, even though the emotions may feel intense, there is an opening of the hearts, and you can feel the energy between you flow. You feel compassion towards them.

It is important also to take care of yourself and know your capacity and limits. If you have been present with someone for a long time, you might start to feel restless. If you are connected, grounded, and present you may also be drawing down a lot of light and healing energy which can leave you feeling charged, wired, or tired.

Realigning Exercise:
Are You Okay?

Next time you ask someone, "How are you?" or "Are you okay?" see if you can feel if what they are saying matches how you feel they are feeling.

Does it feel like they are telling you the truth, telling you what they think you want to hear, being dismissive, or playing it down?

Watch for the two most common emotional bypass words, *fine* and *okay*, as they may be feeling anything but!

I often ask variants of "Is that, 'I feel like crap' fine?", "'I don't know how I feel' fine?", "'I don't want to talk about it' fine?", "'I don't want to be a bother' fine?", or "'Nobody cares' fine?"

Remember people are predominately looking for connection. See if you can create that connection and show that you are genuinely interested in how they are and that you have time to hear them out (if you don't, maybe make another time to connect).

Refer to the previous exercise: How to Be Present with Another in Emotional Crisis.

Realigning Exercise:
Listening — Checklist

Do you know how to truly feel and accept another?

Are you able to *truly* listen to another? Are you able to be present to what they are saying and feeling *without* thinking about what you want to say or how you think you should respond to what they are saying?

Are you able to simply allow them to speak, cry, or be in pain and not feel that you need to fix it or stop it?

Can you be with someone without making judgements in your head about how they are feeling or what they are saying?

Can you listen and just allow it all to wash through you, to feel what they are feeling without commentary?

Are you able to feel them and feel your own feelings?

Are you able to be comfortable (or uncomfortably comfortable) with and in the discomfort of their feelings (because we need to be able to do this to be witness and truly present with another)?

It's important to be present enough to feel how we are feeling in the presence of another. It is not about losing ourselves in another; it is about feeling where and how we meet.

Conclusion

For me, the most valuable information has been "everything is energy," and although saying relationships are just energetic exchanges may sound very cold and clinical, it has helped transform and deepen my relationships. I can accept others for who or how they are more easily and naturally and can see my role in how others are relating to me. With presence to realign the energy, the whole dance changes.

Although reading this book may have been helpful, maybe even transformative, the real power is in doing the work. You may not see changes immediately or feel you are getting results, but please do not let it discourage you. Sometimes things take time to integrate. Encourage yourself as you do this work, because it takes courage to look at yourself and others with loving honesty.

When you catch yourself replaying old habits, do not judge, berate, or belittle yourself. Instead, congratulate yourself! YOU NOTICED! Even if it was later, noticing is where change starts.

Just because I have written this book, do not be fooled into thinking I have my life sorted or even that I remember to use these tools in the moment. I have walked around with pain for days, only to remember the tools which could help me and that I could have applied and used earlier. I believe sometimes it is also a timing thing and it may not have worked earlier.

I still experience bad days, struggle with self-confidence, and sabotage my efforts – however it is improving. One thing I firmly stand by, is that it is worth the work. My life and health are leagues away from where I started. Yes, I still have rare moments of "stop the world I want to get off," but I am noticing it is often my child-self saying, "It's too overwhelming," and so I sit with this younger child version of me and listen and feel... until she wants to run off and play.

As much as we might wish some things would just go away and never return, it may not happen; however, with acceptance—whether it stays or goes—it does not have to rule our life or rob our joy. We can reclaim our power from those experiences that have been leaching or robbing us blind.

Here is your doggy bag of goodies and key points to take home:

- Everything is energy and consciousness.
- You are powerful beyond your wildest imagination.
- Embrace your uniqueness and your commonality.
- Be aware of how or where you are being conditioned (not yourself).
- The words you use and stories you tell have enormous power; consciously changing your words and story can change your life.
- You deserve love and joy in your life.
- Be self-responsible; bring your power back.
- Trust your intuition and trust yourself with your own life.
- Maintain your freedom of choice.
- Forgiveness is the most powerful transformative energy; forgive yourself.
- Do you want to be right or happy?
- Ask for divine assistance and divine timing.
- THE most important relationship is the one you have with yourself (as no matter where you go, there you are!).
- It is not a question of what it is: Are you aligned with it?
- Learn to truly listen to yourself and others.
- Be kind, gentle, tender, encouraging, and loving towards yourself.

This book is the first of a three-part series. In the next book I cover health and well-being, providing practical information and exercises to realign with your healthier vital joyous self. Learn the ten basic principles of health and well-being and how to realign with perfect health.

You live in an absolutely amazing body which has miraculous abilities to heal. Learning how to reconnect with that is vital, as sometimes we simply interfere too much and focus on things that hinder rather than heal.

Thank you for taking the time to read this book and for allowing me to share my experiences and knowledge with you. I trust there was something in here that has inspired, nurtured, or activated you.

May you be filled with joy, love, and peace.

Enjoy

XX

Appendix I: Realigning Exercises

About the Author

Angela, a science graduate, felt incomplete with her studies and chose to move from the country to the city to "make it in the real world." Even though she achieved success in the outer world (career and money), her inner world and health collapsed.

Unable to find answers to her health struggles and burnout, Angela's intuitive and scientific mind began to formulate the solutions she desired. Drawing on numerous alternative health modalities, she saw key patterns to realign illness and disease in the body and restore harmony and wellness.

She empowers women who struggle with anxiety, self-doubt, confidence and trusting their intuition to work with the wisdom of their emotions, so they can listen to their body, improve self-care and live from their authenticity.

Her simple system, Realigning Self, disentangles and heals the programming and patterns that hold you back from being yourself, reconnecting and trusting your intuitive gifts, and living from greater vitality, well-being, and joy.

There are many ways to connect with Angela:

Website:
https://realigningself.com.au/

Courses on Teachable:
https://realigning-self.teachable.com/

YouTube:
https://www.youtube.com/@realigningself

Facebook:
https://www.facebook.com/groups/4202125259853628

LinkedIn:

https://au.linkedin.com/in/angela-anderson-34b57028

For free gifts, cheat sheets, summary downloads, and access to the REALigning SELF course:

For more great books from Peak Press
Visit Books.GracePointPublishing.com

PEAK PRESS

If you enjoyed reading *Realign with Joy,* and purchased it through an online retailer, please return to the site and write a review to help others find the book.

www.ingramcontent.com/pod-product-compliance
Lightning Source LLC
Chambersburg PA
CBHW052033090426
42739CB00010B/1883